Poems of Adam Lindsay Gordon

Adam Lindsay Gordon

Esprios.com

POEMS

By

ADAM LINDSAY GORDON

[British-born Australian Steeple-Chase Rider and Poet—1833-1870.]

1893

Sea Spray and Smoke Drift
Bush Ballads & Galloping Rhymes
Miscellaneous Poems
Ashtaroth: A Dramatic Lyric

CONTENTS

IN MEMORIAM.
PREFACE.
SEA SPRAY AND SMOKE DRIFT
Podas Okus
Gone
Unshriven
Ye Wearie Wayfarer, hys Ballad In Eight Fyttes.
Borrow'd Plumes
A Legend of Madrid
Fauconshawe
Rippling Water
Cui Bono
Bellona
The Song of the Surf
Whisperings in Wattle-Boughs
Confiteor
Sunlight on the Sea
Delilah
From Lightning and Tempest
Wormwood and Nightshade
Ars Longa
The Last Leap
Quare Fatigasti

HIPPODROMANIA; OR, WHIFFS FROM THE PIPE
The Roll of the Kettledrum; or, The Lay of the Last Charger

BUSH BALLADS & GALLOPING RHYMES
The Sick Stockrider
The Swimmer
From the Wreck
No Name
Wolf and Hound
De Te

How we Beat the Favourite
Fragmentary Scenes from the Road to Avernus
Doubtful Dreams
The Rhyme of Joyous Garde
Thora's Song
The Three Friends
A Song of Autumn
The Romance of Britomarte
Laudamus
A Basket of Flowers
A Fragment
MISCELLANEOUS POEMS
"The Old Leaven"
An Exile's Farewell
"Early Adieux"
A Hunting Song
To a Proud Beauty
Thick-headed Thoughts

ASHTAROTH: A Dramatic Lyric
FOOTNOTES:

In Memoriam.
(A. L. Gordon.)

At rest! Hard by the margin of that sea
Whose sounds are mingled with his noble verse,
Now lies the shell that never more will house
The fine, strong spirit of my gifted friend.
Yea, he who flashed upon us suddenly,
A shining soul with syllables of fire,
Who sang the first great songs these lands can claim
To be their own; the one who did not seem
To know what royal place awaited him
Within the Temple of the Beautiful,
Has passed away; and we who knew him, sit
Aghast in darkness, dumb with that great grief,
Whose stature yet we cannot comprehend;
While over yonder churchyard, hearsed with pines,
The night-wind sings its immemorial hymn,
And sobs above a newly-covered grave.

The bard, the scholar, and the man who lived
That frank, that open-hearted life which keeps
The splendid fire of English chivalry
From dying out; the one who never wronged
A fellow-man; the faithful friend who judged
The many, anxious to be loved of him,
By what he saw, and not by what he heard,
As lesser spirits do; the brave great soul
That never told a lie, or turned aside
To fly from danger; he, I say, was one
Of that bright company this sin-stained world
Can ill afford to lose.

    They did not know,
The hundreds who had read his sturdy verse,
And revelled over ringing major notes,
The mournful meaning of the undersong
Which runs through all he wrote, and often takes
The deep autumnal, half-prophetic tone
Of forest winds in March; nor did they think

That on that healthy-hearted man there lay
The wild specific curse which seems to cling
For ever to the Poet's twofold life!

To Adam Lindsay Gordon, I who laid
Two years ago on Lionel Michael's grave
A tender leaf of my regard; yea I,
Who culled a garland from the flowers of song
To place where Harpur sleeps; I, left alone,
The sad disciple of a shining band
Now gone! to Adam Lindsay Gordon's name
I dedicate these lines; and if 'tis true
That, past the darkness of the grave, the soul
Becomes omniscient, then the bard may stoop
From his high seat to take the offering,
And read it with a sigh for human friends,
In human bonds, and gray with human griefs.

And having wove and proffered this poor wreath,
I stand to-day as lone as he who saw
At nightfall through the glimmering moony mists,
The last of Arthur on the wailing mere,
And strained in vain to hear the going voice.

    Henry Kendall.

Preface.

The poems of Gordon have an interest beyond the mere personal one which his friends attach to his name. Written, as they were, at odd times and leisure moments of a stirring and adventurous life, it is not to be wondered at if they are unequal or unfinished. The astonishment of those who knew the man, and can gauge the capacity of this city to foster poetic instinct, is that such work was ever produced here at all. Intensely nervous, and feeling much of that shame at the exercise of the higher intelligence which besets those who are known to be renowned in field sports, Gordon produced his poems shyly, scribbled them on scraps of paper, and sent them anonymously to magazines. It was not until he discovered one morning that everybody knew a couplet or two of "How we Beat the Favourite" that he consented to forego his anonymity and appear in the unsuspected character of a versemaker. The success of his republished "collected" poems gave him courage, and the unreserved praise which greeted "Bush Ballads" should have urged him to forget or to conquer those evil promptings which, unhappily, brought about his untimely death.

Adam Lindsay Gordon was the son of an officer in the English army, and was educated at Woolwich, in order that he might follow the profession of his family. At the time when he was a cadet there was no sign of either of the two great wars which were about to call forth the strength of English arms, and, like many other men of his day, he quitted his prospects of service and emigrated. He went to South Australia and started as a sheep farmer. His efforts were attended with failure. He lost his capital, and, owning nothing but a love for horsemanship and a head full of Browning and Shelley, plunged into the varied life which gold-mining, "overlanding", and cattle-driving affords. From this experience he emerged to light in Melbourne as the best amateur steeplechase rider in the colonies. The victory he won for Major Baker in 1868, when he rode Babbler for the Cup Steeplechase, made him popular, and the almost simultaneous publication of his last volume of poems gave him welcome entrance to the houses of all who had pretensions to literary taste. The reputation of the book spread to England, and Major Whyte Melville did not disdain to place the lines of the dashing Australian author at the head of his own dashing descriptions of sporting scenery. Unhappily, the melancholy which Gordon's friends had with pain observed increased daily, and in the full flood of his success, with congratulations pouring upon him from every side, he was found dead in the heather near his home with a bullet from his own rifle in his brain.

I do not propose to criticise the volumes which these few lines of preface introduce to the reader. The influence of Browning and of Swinburne upon the writer's taste is plain. There is plainly visible also, however, a keen sense for natural beauty and a manly admiration for healthy living. If in "Ashtaroth" and "Bellona" we recognise the swing of a familiar metre, in such poems as "The Sick Stockrider" we perceive the genuine poetic instinct united to a very clear perception of the loveliness of duty and of labour.

>"'Twas merry in the glowing morn, among the gleaming grass,
> To wander as we've wandered many a mile,
> And blow the cool tobacco cloud, and watch the white wreaths pass,
> Sitting loosely in the saddle all the while;
> 'Twas merry 'mid the blackwoods, when we spied the station roofs,
> To wheel the wild scrub cattle at the yard,
> With a running fire of stockwhips and a fiery run of hoofs,
> Oh! the hardest day was never then too hard!
>
> "Aye! we had a glorious gallop after 'Starlight' and his gang,
> When they bolted from Sylvester's on the flat;
> How the sun-dried reed-beds crackled, how the flint-strewn ranges rang
> To the strokes of 'Mountaineer' and 'Acrobat';
> Hard behind them in the timber, harder still across the heath,
> Close behind them through the tea-tree scrub we dashed;
> And the golden-tinted fern leaves, how they rustled underneath!
> And the honeysuckle osiers, how they crash'd!"

This is genuine. There is no "poetic evolution from the depths of internal consciousness" here. The writer has ridden his ride as well as written it.

The student of these unpretending volumes will be repaid for his labour. He will find in them something very like the beginnings of a national school of Australian poetry. In historic Europe, where every rood of ground is hallowed in legend and in song, the least imaginative can find food for sad and sweet reflection. When strolling at noon down an English country lane, lounging at sunset by some ruined chapel on the margin of an Irish lake, or watching the mists of morning unveil Ben Lomond, we feel all the charm which springs from association with the past. Soothed, saddened, and cheered by turns, we partake of the varied moods which belong not so much to ourselves as to the dead men who, in old days, sung, suffered, or conquered in the scenes which we survey. But this our native or adopted land has no past, no story. No poet speaks to us. Do we need a poet to interpret Nature's teachings, we must look into our own hearts, if perchance we may find a poet there.

What is the dominant note of Australian scenery? That which is the dominant note of Edgar Allan Poe's poetry — Weird Melancholy. A poem like "L'Allegro" could never be written by an Australian. It is too airy, too sweet, too freshly happy. The Australian mountain forests are funereal, secret, stern. Their solitude is desolation. They seem to stifle, in their black gorges, a story of sullen despair. No tender sentiment is nourished in their shade. In other lands the dying year is mourned, the falling leaves drop lightly on his bier. In the Australian forests no leaves fall. The savage winds shout among the rock clefts. From the melancholy gums strips of white bark hang and rustle. The very animal life of these frowning hills is either grotesque or ghostly. Great grey kangaroos hop noiselessly over the coarse grass. Flights of white cockatoos stream out, shrieking like evil souls. The sun suddenly sinks, and the mopokes burst out into horrible peals of semi-human laughter. The natives aver that, when night comes, from out the bottomless depth of some lagoon the Bunyip rises, and, in form like monstrous sea-calf, drags his loathsome length from out the ooze. From a corner of the silent forest rises a dismal chant, and around a fire dance natives painted like skeletons. All is fear-inspiring and gloomy. No bright fancies are linked with the memories of the mountains. Hopeless explorers have named them out of their sufferings — Mount Misery, Mount Dreadful, Mount Despair. As when among sylvan scenes in places

"Made green with the running of rivers,
And gracious with temperate air, "

the soul is soothed and satisfied, so, placed before the frightful grandeur of these barren hills, it drinks in their sentiment of defiant ferocity, and is steeped in bitterness.

Australia has rightly been named the Land of the Dawning. Wrapped in the midst of early morning, her history looms vague and gigantic. The lonely horseman riding between the moonlight and the day sees vast shadows creeping across the shelterless and silent plains, hears strange noises in the primeval forest, where flourishes a vegetation long dead in other lands, and feels, despite his fortune, that the trim utilitarian civilisation which bred him shrinks into insignificance beside the contemptuous grandeur of forest and ranges coeval with an age in which European scientists have cradled his own race.

There is a poem in every form of tree or flower, but the poetry which lives in the trees and flowers of Australia differs from those of other countries. Europe is the home of knightly song, of bright deeds and clear morning thought. Asia sinks beneath the weighty recollections of her past magnificence, as the Suttee sinks, jewel burdened, upon the corpse of dread grandeur, destructive even in its death. America swiftly hurries on her way, rapid, glittering, insatiable even as one of her own giant waterfalls. From the jungles of Africa, and the creeper-tangled groves of the Islands of the South, arise, from the glowing hearts of a thousand flowers, heavy and intoxicating odours — the Upas-poison which dwells in barbaric sensuality. In Australia alone is to be found the Grotesque, the Weird, the strange scribblings of Nature learning how to write. Some see no beauty in our trees without shade, our flowers without perfume, our birds who cannot fly, and our beasts who have not yet learned to walk on all fours. But the dweller in the wilderness acknowledges the subtle charm of this fantastic land of monstrosities. He becomes familiar with the beauty of loneliness. Whispered to by the myriad tongues of the wilderness, he learns the language of the barren and the uncouth, and can read the hieroglyphics of haggard gum-trees, blown into odd shapes, distorted with fierce hot winds, or cramped with cold nights, when the Southern Cross freezes in a cloudless sky of icy blue. The phantasmagoria of that wild dreamland termed the Bush interprets itself, and the Poet of our desolation begins to comprehend why free Esau loved his heritage of desert sand better than all the bountiful richness of Egypt.

Marcus Clarke.

Poems of Adam Lindsay Gordon

Sea Spray and Smoke Drift

Podas Okus

Am I waking? Was I sleeping?
 Dearest, are you watching yet?
Traces on your cheeks of weeping
 Glitter, 'tis in vain you fret;
Drifting ever! drifting onward!
 In the glass the bright sand runs
Steadily and slowly downward;
 Hushed are all the Myrmidons.

Has Automedon been banish'd
 From his post beside my bed?
Where has Agamemnon vanished?
 Where is warlike Diomed?
Where is Nestor? where Ulysses?
 Menelaus, where is he?
Call them not, more dear your kisses
 Than their prosings are to me.

Daylight fades and night must follow,
 Low, where sea and sky combine,
Droops the orb of great Apollo,
 Hostile god to me and mine.
Through the tent's wide entrance streaming,
 In a flood of glory rare,
Glides the golden sunset, gleaming
 On your golden, gleaming hair.

Chide him not, the leech who tarries,
 Surest aid were all too late;
Surer far the shaft of Paris,
 Winged by Phoebus and by fate;
When he crouch'd behind the gable,
 Had I once his features scann'd,

Phoebus' self had scarce been able
 To have nerved his trembling hand.

Blue-eyed maiden! dear Athena!
 Goddess chaste, and wise and brave,
From the snares of Polyxena
 Thou would'st fain thy favourite save.
Tell me, is it not far better
 That it should be as it is?
Jove's behest we cannot fetter,
 Fate's decrees are always his.

Many seek for peace and riches,
 Length of days and life of ease;
I have sought for one thing, which is
 Fairer unto me than these.
Often, too, I've heard the story,
 In my boyhood, of the doom
Which the fates assigned me — Glory,
 Coupled with an early tomb.

Swift assault and sudden sally
 Underneath the Trojan wall;
Charge, and countercharge, and rally,
 War-cry loud, and trumpet call;
Doubtful strain of desp'rate battle,
 Cut and thrust and grapple fierce,
Swords that ring on shields that rattle,
 Blades that gash and darts that pierce; —

I have done with these for ever;
 By the loud resounding sea,
Where the reedy jav'lins quiver,
 There is now no place for me.
Day by day our ranks diminish,
 We are falling day by day;
But our sons the strife will finish,
 Where man tarries man must slay.

Life, 'tis said, to all men sweet is,
 Death to all must bitter be;
Wherefore thus, oh, mother Thetis!
 None can baffle Jove's decree?

I am ready, I am willing,
 To resign my stormy life;
Weary of this long blood-spilling,
 Sated with this ceaseless strife.

Shorter doom I've pictured dimly,
 On a bed of crimson sand;
Fighting hard and dying grimly,
 Silent lips, and striking hand.
But the toughest lives are brittle,
 And the bravest and the best
Lightly fall — it matters little;
 Now I only long for rest.

I have seen enough of slaughter,
 Seen Scamander's torrent red,
Seen hot blood poured out like water,
 Seen the champaign heaped with dead.
Men will call me unrelenting,
 Pitiless, vindictive, stern;
Few will raise a voice dissenting,
 Few will better things discern.

Speak! the fires of life are reeling,
 Like the wildfires on the marsh,
Was I to a friend unfeeling?
 Was I to a mistress harsh?
Was there nought save bloodshed throbbing
 In this heart and on this brow?
Whisper! girl, in silence sobbing!
 Dead Patroclus! answer thou!

Dry those violet orbs that glisten,
 Darling, I have had my day;
Place your hand in mine and listen,
 Ere the strong soul cleaves its way
Through the death mist hovering o'er me,
 As the stout ship cleaves the wave,
To my fathers gone before me,
 To the gods who love the brave!

Courage, we must part for certain;
 Shades that sink and shades that rise,

Blending in a shroud-like curtain,
  Gather o'er these weary eyes.
O'er the fields we used to roam, in
  Brighter days and lighter cheer,
Gathers thus the quiet gloaming —
  Now, I ween, the end is near.

For the hand that clasps your fingers,
  Closing in the death-grip tight,
Scarcely feels the warmth that lingers,
  Scarcely heeds the pressure light;
While the failing pulse that alters,
  Changing 'neath a death chill damp,
Flickers, flutters, flags, and falters,
  Feebly like a waning lamp.

Think'st thou, love, 'twill chafe my ghost in
  Hades' realm, where heroes shine,
Should I hear the shepherd boasting
  To his Argive concubine?
Let him boast, the girlish victor,
  Let him brag; not thus, I trow,
Were the laurels torn from Hector,
  Not so very long ago.

Does my voice sound thick and husky?
  Is my hand no longer warm?
Round that neck where pearls look dusky
  Let me once more wind my arm;
Rest my head upon that shoulder,
  Where it rested oft of yore;
Warm and white, yet seeming colder
  Now than e'er it seem'd before.

'Twas the fraud of Priam's daughter,
  Not the force of Priam's son,
Slew me — ask not why I sought her,
  'Twas my doom — her work is done!
Fairer far than she, and dearer,
  By a thousandfold thou art;
Come, my own one, nestle nearer,
  Cheating death of half his smart.

Slowly, while your amber tresses
 Shower down their golden rain,
Let me drink those last caresses,
 Never to be felt again;
Yet th' Elysian halls are spacious,
 Somewhere near me I may keep
Room — who knows? — The gods are gracious;
 Lay me lower — let me sleep!

Lower yet, my senses wander,
 And my spirit seems to roll
With the tide of swift Scamander
 Rushing to a viewless goal.
In my ears, like distant washing
 Of the surf upon the shore,
Drones a murmur, faintly splashing,
 'Tis the splash of Charon's oar.

Lower yet, my own Briseis,
 Denser shadows veil the light;
Hush, what is to be, to be is,
 Close my eyes, and say good-night.
Lightly lay your red lips, kissing,
 On this cold mouth, while your thumbs
Lie on these cold eyelids pressing —
 Pallas! thus thy soldier comes!

Gone

In Collins-street standeth a statue tall — *
 A statue tall on a pillar of stone,
Telling its story, to great and small,
 Of the dust reclaimed from the sand waste lone.
Weary and wasted, and worn and wan,
 Feeble and faint, and languid and low,
He lay on the desert a dying man,
 Who has gone, my friends, where we all must go.

There are perils by land, and perils by water,
 Short, I ween, are the obsequies
Of the landsman lost, but they may be shorter
 With the mariner lost in the trackless seas;
And well for him when the timbers start,
 And the stout ship reels and settles below,
Who goes to his doom with as bold a heart
 As that dead man gone where we all must go.

Man is stubborn his rights to yield,
 And redder than dews at eventide
Are the dews of battle, shed on the field,
 By a nation's wrath or a despot's pride;
But few who have heard their death-knell roll,
 From the cannon's lips where they faced the foe,
Have fallen as stout and steady of soul
 As that dead man gone where we all must go.

Traverse yon spacious burial-ground,
 Many are sleeping soundly there,
Who pass'd with mourners standing around,
 Kindred and friends, and children fair;
Did he envy such ending? 'twere hard to say;
 Had he cause to envy such ending? no;
Can the spirit feel for the senseless clay
 When it once has gone where we all must go?

What matters the sand or the whitening chalk,
 The blighted herbage, the black'ning log,
The crooked beak of the eagle-hawk,
 Or the hot red tongue of the native dog?
That couch was rugged, those sextons rude,
 Yet, in spite of a leaden shroud, we know
That the bravest and fairest are earth-worms' food,
 When once they've gone where we all must go.

With the pistol clenched in his failing hand,
 With the death mist spread o'er his fading eyes,
He saw the sun go down on the sand,
 And he slept, and never saw it rise;
'Twas well; he toil'd till his task was done,
 Constant and calm in his latest throe;
The storm was weathered, the battle was won,
 When he went, my friends, where we all must go.

God grant that whenever, soon or late,
 Our course is run and our goal is reach'd,
We may meet our fate as steady and straight
 As he whose bones in yon desert bleach'd;
No tears are needed — our cheeks are dry,
 We have none to waste upon living woe;
Shall we sigh for one who has ceased to sigh,
 Having gone, my friends, where we all must go?

We tarry yet, we are toiling still,
 He is gone and he fares the best,
He fought against odds, he struggled up hill,
 He has fairly earned his season of rest;
No tears are needed — fill out the wine,
 Let the goblets clash, and the grape juice flow;
Ho! pledge me a death-drink, comrade mine,
 To a brave man gone where we all must go.

* The extension of the tramways has necessitated the removal of this statue to Spring-street.

Unshriven

Oh! the sun rose on the lea, and the bird sang merrilie,
  And the steed stood ready harness'd in the hall,
And he left his lady's bower, and he sought the eastern tower,
  And he lifted cloak and weapon from the wall.

"We were wed but yester-noon, must we separate so soon?
  Must you travel unassoiled and, aye, unshriven,
With the blood stain on your hand, and the red streak on your
    brand,
  And your guilt all unconfessed and unforgiven?"

"Tho' it were but yester-even we were wedded, still unshriven,
  Across the moor this morning I must ride;
I must gallop fast and straight, for my errand will not wait;
  Fear naught, I shall return at eventide."

"If I fear, it is for thee, thy weal is dear to me,
  Yon moor with retribution seemeth rife;
As we've sown so must we reap, and I've started in my sleep
  At the voice of the avenger, `Life for life'."

"My arm is strong, I ween, and my trusty blade is keen,
  And the courser that I ride is swift and sure,
And I cannot break my oath, though to leave thee I am loth,
  There is one that I must meet upon the moor."

 *   *   *   *   *

Oh! the sun shone on the lea, and the bird sang merrilie,
  Down the avenue and through the iron gate,
Spurr'd and belted, so he rode, steel to draw and steel to goad,
  And across the moor he galloped fast and straight.

 *   *   *   *   *

 *   *   *   *   *

Oh! the sun shone on the lea, and the bird sang full of glee,
　Ere the mists of evening gather'd chill and grey;
But the wild bird's merry note on the deaf ear never smote,
　And the sunshine never warmed the lifeless clay.

Ere the sun began to droop, or the mist began to stoop,
　The youthful bride lay swooning in the hall;
Empty saddle on his back, broken bridle hanging slack,
　The steed returned full gallop to the stall.

Oh! the sun sank in the sea, and the wind wailed drearilie;
　Let the bells in yonder monastery toll,
For the night rack nestles dark round the body stiff and stark,
　And unshriven to its Maker flies the soul.

Ye Wearie Wayfarer, hys Ballad
In Eight Fyttes.

Fytte I
By Wood and Wold
[A Preamble]

"Beneath the greenwood bough." — W. Scott.

Lightly the breath of the spring wind blows,
 Though laden with faint perfume,
'Tis the fragrance rare that the bushman knows,
 The scent of the wattle bloom.
Two-thirds of our journey at least are done,
 Old horse! let us take a spell
In the shade from the glare of the noonday sun,
 Thus far we have travell'd well;
Your bridle I'll slip, your saddle ungirth,
 And lay them beside this log,
For you'll roll in that track of reddish earth,
 And shake like a water-dog.

Upon yonder rise there's a clump of trees —
 Their shadows look cool and broad —
You can crop the grass as fast as you please,
 While I stretch my limbs on the sward;
'Tis pleasant, I ween, with a leafy screen
 O'er the weary head, to lie
On the mossy carpet of emerald green,
 'Neath the vault of the azure sky;
Thus all alone by the wood and wold,
 I yield myself once again
To the memories old that, like tales fresh told,
 Come flitting across the brain.

Fytte II
By Flood and Field
[A Legend of the Cottiswold]

"They have saddled a hundred milk-white steeds,
They have bridled a hundred black." — Old Ballad.
"He turned in his saddle, now follow who dare.
I ride for my country, quoth * *." — Lawrence.

I remember the lowering wintry morn,
  And the mist on the Cotswold hills,
Where I once heard the blast of the huntsman's horn,
  Not far from the seven rills.
Jack Esdale was there, and Hugh St. Clair,
  Bob Chapman and Andrew Kerr,
And big George Griffiths on Devil-May-Care,
  And — black Tom Oliver.
And one who rode on a dark-brown steed,
  Clean jointed, sinewy, spare,
With the lean game head of the Blacklock breed,
And the resolute eye that loves the lead,
  And the quarters massive and square —
A tower of strength, with a promise of speed
  (There was Celtic blood in the pair).

I remember how merry a start we got,
  When the red fox broke from the gorse,
In a country so deep, with a scent so hot,
  That the hound could outpace the horse;
I remember how few in the front rank shew'd,
  How endless appeared the tail,
On the brown hill-side, where we cross'd the road,
  And headed towards the vale.
The dark-brown steed on the left was there,
  On the right was a dappled grey,
And between the pair, on a chestnut mare,
  The duffer who writes this lay.
What business had "this child" there to ride?
  But little or none at all;
Yet I held my own for a while in "the pride
  That goeth before a fall."

Though rashness can hope for but one result,
 We are heedless when fate draws nigh us,
And the maxim holds good, "Quem perdere vult
 Deus, dementat prius."

The right hand man to the left hand said,
 As down in the vale we went,
"Harden your heart like a millstone, Ned,
 And set your face as flint;
Solid and tall is the rasping wall
 That stretches before us yonder;
You must have it at speed or not at all,
 'Twere better to halt than to ponder,
For the stream runs wide on the take-off side,
 And washes the clay bank under;
Here goes for a pull, 'tis a madman's ride,
 And a broken neck if you blunder."

No word in reply his comrade spoke,
 Nor waver'd nor once look'd round,
But I saw him shorten his horse's stroke
 As we splash'd through the marshy ground;
I remember the laugh that all the while
 On his quiet features play'd: —
So he rode to his death, with that careless smile,
 In the van of the "Light Brigade";
So stricken by Russian grape, the cheer
 Rang out, while he toppled back,
From the shattered lungs as merry and clear
 As it did when it roused the pack.
Let never a tear his memory stain,
 Give his ashes never a sigh,
One of many who perished, NOT IN VAIN,
 AS A TYPE OF OUR CHIVALRY —

I remember one thrust he gave to his hat,
 And two to the flanks of the brown,
And still as a statue of old he sat,
 And he shot to the front, hands down;
I remember the snort and the stag-like bound
 Of the steed six lengths to the fore,
And the laugh of the rider while, landing sound,
 He turned in his saddle and glanced around;

I remember — but little more,
Save a bird's-eye gleam of the dashing stream,
 A jarring thud on the wall,
A shock and the blank of a nightmare's dream —
 I was down with a stunning fall.

Fytte III
Zu der edlen Yagd
[A Treatise on Trees — Vine-tree v. Saddle-tree]

"Now, welcome, welcome, masters mine,
 Thrice welcome to the noble chase,
Nor earthly sport, nor sport divine,
 Can take such honourable place." — Ballad of the Wild Huntsman.
            (Free Translation.)

I remember some words my father said,
 When I was an urchin vain; —
God rest his soul, in his narrow bed
 These ten long years he hath lain.
When I think one drop of the blood he bore
 This faint heart surely must hold,
It may be my fancy and nothing more,
 But the faint heart seemeth bold.

He said that as from the blood of grape,
 Or from juice distilled from the grain,
False vigour, soon to evaporate,
 Is lent to nerve and brain,
So the coward will dare on the gallant horse
 What he never would dare alone,
Because he exults in a borrowed force,
 And a hardihood not his own.

And it may be so, yet this difference lies
 'Twixt the vine and the saddle-tree,
The spurious courage that drink supplies
 Sets our baser passions free;
But the stimulant which the horseman feels

When he gallops fast and straight,
To his better nature most appeals,
 And charity conquers hate.

As the kindly sunshine thaws the snow,
 E'en malice and spite will yield,
We could almost welcome our mortal foe
 In the saddle by flood and field;
And chivalry dawns in the merry tale
 That "Market Harborough" writes,
And the yarns of "Nimrod" and "Martingale"
 Seem legends of loyal knights.

Now tell me for once, old horse of mine,
 Grazing round me loose and free,
Does your ancient equine heart repine
 For a burst in such companie,
Where "the POWERS that be" in the front rank ride,
 To hold your own with the throng,
Or to plunge at "Faugh-a-Ballagh's" side
 In the rapids of Dandenong.

Don't tread on my toes, you're no foolish weight,
 So I found to my cost, as under
Your carcase I lay, when you rose too late,
 Yet I blame you not for the blunder.
What! sulky old man, your under-lip falls!
 You think I, too, ready to rail am
At your kinship remote to that duffer at walls,
 The talkative roadster of Balaam.

Fytte IV
In Utrumque Paratus
[A Logical Discussion]

"Then hey for boot and horse, lad!
 And round the world away!
Young blood will have its course, lad!
 And every dog his day!" — C. Kingsley.

14

There's a formula which the west country clowns
 Once used, ere their blows fell thick,
At the fairs on the Devon and Cornwall downs,
 In their bouts with the single-stick.
You may read a moral, not far amiss,
 If you care to moralise,
In the crossing-guard, where the ash-plants kiss,
 To the words "God spare our eyes".
No game was ever yet worth a rap
 For a rational man to play,
Into which no accident, no mishap,
 Could possibly find its way.

If you hold the willow, a shooter from Wills
 May transform you into a hopper,
And the football meadow is rife with spills,
 If you feel disposed for a cropper;
In a rattling gallop with hound and horse
 You may chance to reverse the medal
On the sward, with the saddle your loins across,
 And your hunter's loins on the saddle;
In the stubbles you'll find it hard to frame
 A remonstrance firm, yet civil,
When oft as "our mutual friend" takes aim,
Long odds may be laid on the rising game,
 And against your gaiters level;
There's danger even where fish are caught,
 To those who a wetting fear;
For what's worth having must aye be bought,
And sport's like life and life's like sport,
 "It ain't all skittles and beer."

The honey bag lies close to the sting,
 The rose is fenced by the thorn,
Shall we leave to others their gathering,
And turn from clustering fruits that cling
 To the garden wall in scorn?
Albeit those purple grapes hang high,
 Like the fox in the ancient tale,
Let us pause and try, ere we pass them by,
 Though we, like the fox, may fail.

All hurry is worse than useless; think

On the adage, "'Tis pace that kills";
Shun bad tobacco, avoid strong drink,
 Abstain from Holloway's pills,
Wear woollen socks, they're the best you'll find,
 Beware how you leave off flannel;
And whatever you do, don't change your mind
 When once you have picked your panel;
With a bank of cloud in the south south-east,
 Stand ready to shorten sail;
Fight shy of a corporation feast;
 Don't trust to a martingale;
Keep your powder dry, and shut one eye,
 Not both, when you touch your trigger;
Don't stop with your head too frequently
 (This advice ain't meant for a nigger);
Look before you leap, if you like, but if
 You mean leaping, don't look long,
Or the weakest place will soon grow stiff,
 And the strongest doubly strong;
As far as you can, to every man,
 Let your aid be freely given,
And hit out straight, 'tis your shortest plan,
 When against the ropes you're driven.

Mere pluck, though not in the least sublime,
 Is wiser than blank dismay,
Since "No sparrow can fall before its time",
 And we're valued higher than they;
So hope for the best and leave the rest
 In charge of a stronger hand,
Like the honest boors in the far-off west,
 With the formula terse and grand.

They were men for the most part rough and rude,
 Dull and illiterate,
But they nursed no quarrel, they cherished no feud,
 They were strangers to spite and hate;
In a kindly spirit they took their stand,
 That brothers and sons might learn
How a man should uphold the sports of his land,
And strike his best with a strong right hand,
 And take his strokes in return.
"'Twas a barbarous practice," the Quaker cries,

"'Tis a thing of the past, thank heaven" —
Keep your thanks till the combative instinct dies
  With the taint of the olden leaven;
Yes, the times are changed, for better or worse,
  The prayer that no harm befall
Has given its place to a drunken curse,
  And the manly game to a brawl.

Our burdens are heavy, our natures weak,
  Some pastime devoid of harm
May we look for? "Puritan elder, speak!"
  "Yea, friend, peradventure thou mayest seek
  Recreation singing a psalm."
If I did, your visage so grim and stern
  Would relax in a ghastly smile,
For of music I never one note could learn,
And my feeble minstrelsy would turn
  Your chant to discord vile.

Tho' the Philistine's mail could not avail,
  Nor the spear like a weaver's beam,
There are episodes yet in the Psalmist's tale,
To obliterate which his poems fail,
  Which his exploits fail to redeem.
Can the Hittite's wrongs forgotten be?
Does HE warble "Non nobis Domine",
With his monarch in blissful concert, free
  From all malice to flesh inherent;
Zeruiah's offspring, who served so well,
  Yet between the horns of the altar fell —
Does HIS voice the "Quid gloriaris" swell,
  Or the "Quare fremuerunt"?
It may well be thus where DAVID sings,
  And Uriah joins in the chorus,
But while earth to earthy matter clings,
Neither you nor the bravest of Judah's kings
  As a pattern can stand before us.

Fytte V
Lex Talionis
[A Moral Discourse]

"And if there's blood upon his hand,
'Tis but the blood of deer." — W. Scott.

To beasts of the field, and fowls of the air,
　And fish of the sea alike,
Man's hand is ever slow to spare,
　And ever ready to strike;
With a license to kill, and to work our will,
　In season by land or by water,
To our heart's content we may take our fill
　Of the joys we derive from slaughter.

And few, I reckon, our rights gainsay
　In this world of rapine and wrong,
Where the weak and the timid seem lawful prey
　For the resolute and the strong;
Fins, furs, and feathers, they are and were
　For our use and pleasure created,
We can shoot, and hunt, and angle, and snare,
　Unquestioned, if not unsated.

I have neither the will nor the right to blame,
　Yet to many (though not to all)
The sweets of destruction are somewhat tame
　When no personal risks befall;
Our victims suffer but little, we trust
　(Mere guess-work and blank enigma),
If they suffer at all, our field sports must
　Of cruelty bear the stigma.

Shall we, hard-hearted to their fates, thus
　Soft-hearted shrink from our own,
When the measure we mete is meted to us,
　When we reap as we've always sown?
Shall we who for pastime have squander'd life,
　Who are styled "the Lords of Creation",
Recoil from our chance of more equal strife,

And our risk of retaliation?

Though short is the dying pheasant's pain,
 Scant pity you well may spare,
And the partridge slain is a triumph vain,
 And a risk that a child may dare;
You feel, when you lower the smoking gun,
 Some ruth for yon slaughtered hare,
And hit or miss, in your selfish fun
 The widgeon has little share.

But you've no remorseful qualms or pangs
 When you kneel by the grizzly's lair,
On that conical bullet your sole chance hangs,
 'Tis the weak one's advantage fair,
And the shaggy giant's terrific fangs
 Are ready to crush and tear;
Should you miss, one vision of home and friends,
 Five words of unfinished prayer,
Three savage knife stabs, so your sport ends
In the worrying grapple that chokes and rends; —
 Rare sport, at least, for the bear.

Short shrift! sharp fate! dark doom to dree!
 Hard struggle, though quickly ending!
At home or abroad, by land or sea,
 In peace or war, sore trials must be,
And worse may happen to you or to me,
 For none are secure, and none can flee
 From a destiny impending.

Ah! friend, did you think when the LONDON sank,
Timber by timber, plank by plank,
 In a cauldron of boiling surf,
How alone at least, with never a flinch,
In a rally contested inch by inch,
 You could fall on the trampled turf?
When a livid wall of the sea leaps high,
In the lurid light of a leaden sky,
 And bursts on the quarter railing;
While the howling storm-gust seems to vie
With the crash of splintered beams that fly,
Yet fails too oft to smother the cry

Of women and children wailing?

Then those who listen in sinking ships
To despairing sobs from their lov'd one's lips,
 Where the green wave thus slowly shatters,
May long for the crescent-claw that rips
The bison into ribbons and strips,
 And tears the strong elk to tatters.

Oh! sunderings short of body and breath!
Oh! "battle and murder and sudden death!"
 Against which the Liturgy preaches;
By the will of a just, yet a merciful Power,
Less bitter, perchance, in the mystic hour,
When the wings of the shadowy angel lower,
 Than man in his blindness teaches!

Fytte VI
Potters' Clay
[An Allegorical Interlude]

"Nec propter vitam vivendi perdere causas."

Though the pitcher that goes to the sparkling rill
 Too oft gets broken at last,
There are scores of others its place to fill
 When its earth to the earth is cast;
Keep that pitcher at home, let it never roam,
 But lie like a useless clod,
Yet sooner or later the hour will come
 When its chips are thrown to the sod.

Is it wise, then, say, in the waning day,
 When the vessel is crack'd and old,
To cherish the battered potters' clay,
 As though it were virgin gold?
Take care of yourself, dull, boorish elf,
 Though prudent and safe you seem,
Your pitcher will break on the musty shelf,

And mine by the dazzling stream.

Fytte VII
Cito Pede Preterit Aetas
[A Philosophical Dissertation]

"Gillian's dead, God rest her bier —
 How I loved her many years syne;
Marion's married, but I sit here,
Alive and merry at three-score year,
 Dipping my nose in Gascoigne wine." — Wamba's Song —
Thackeray.

A mellower light doth Sol afford,
 His meridian glare has pass'd,
And the trees on the broad and sloping sward
 Their length'ning shadows cast.
"Time flies." The current will be no joke,
 If swollen by recent rain,
To cross in the dark, so I'll have a smoke,
 And then I'll be off again.

What's up, old horse? Your ears you prick,
 And your eager eyeballs glisten;
'Tis the wild dog's note in the tea-tree thick,
 By the river, to which you listen.
With head erect and tail flung out,
 For a gallop you seem to beg,
But I feel the qualm of a chilling doubt,
 As I glance at your fav'rite leg.

Let the dingo rest, 'tis all for the best;
 In this world there's room enough
For him and you and me and the rest,
 And the country is awful rough.
We've had our gallop in days of yore,
 Now down the hill we must run;
Yet at times we long for one gallop more,
 Although it were only one.

Did our spirits quail at a new four-rail,
 Could a "double" double-bank us,
Ere nerve and sinew began to fail
 In the consulship of Plancus?
When our blood ran rapidly, and when
 Our bones were pliant and limber,
Could we stand a merry cross-counter then,
 A slogging fall over timber?

Arcades ambo! Duffers both,
 In our best of days, alas!
(I tell the truth, though to tell it loth)
 'Tis time we were gone to grass;
The young leaves shoot, the sere leaves fall,
 And the old gives way to the new,
While the preacher cries, "'Tis vanity all,
 And vexation of spirit, too."

Now over my head the vapours curl
 From the bowl of the soothing clay,
In the misty forms that eddy and whirl
 My thoughts are flitting away;
Yes, the preacher's right, 'tis vanity all,
 But the sweeping rebuke he showers
On vanities all may heaviest fall
 On vanities worse than ours.

We have no wish to exaggerate
 The worth of the sports we prize,
Some toil for their Church, and some for their State,
 And some for their merchandise;
Some traffic and trade in the city's mart,
 Some travel by land and sea,
Some follow science, some cleave to art,
 And some to scandal and tea;

And some for their country and their queen
 Would fight, if the chance they had,
Good sooth, 'twere a sorry world, I ween,
 If we all went galloping mad;
Yet if once we efface the joys of the chase
 From the land, and outroot the Stud,
GOOD-BYE TO THE ANGLO-SAXON RACE!

FAREWELL TO THE NORMAN BLOOD!

Where the burn runs down to the uplands brown,
 From the heights of the snow-clad range,
What anodyne drawn from the stifling town
 Can be reckon'd a fair exchange
For the stalker's stride, on the mountain side,
 In the bracing northern weather,
To the slopes where couch, in their antler'd pride,
 The deer on the perfum'd heather?

Oh! the vigour with which the air is rife!
 The spirit of joyous motion;
The fever, the fulness of animal life,
 Can be drain'd from no earthly potion!
The lungs with the living gas grow light,
 And the limbs feel the strength of ten,
While the chest expands with its madd'ning might,
 GOD'S GLORIOUS OXYGEN.

Thus the measur'd stroke, on elastic sward,
 Of the steed three parts extended,
Hard held, the breath of his nostrils broad,
 With the golden ether blended;
Then the leap, the rise from the springy turf,
 The rush through the buoyant air,
And the light shock landing — the veriest serf
 Is an emperor then and there!

Such scenes! sensation and sound and sight!
 To some undiscover'd shore
On the current of Time's remorseless flight
 Have they swept to return no more?
While, like phantoms bright of the fever'd night,
 That have vex'd our slumbers of yore,
You follow us still in your ghostly might,
 Dead days that have gone before.

Vain dreams, again and again re-told,
 Must you crowd on the weary brain,
Till the fingers are cold that entwin'd of old
 Round foil and trigger and rein,
Till stay'd for aye are the roving feet,

Till the restless hands are quiet,
Till the stubborn heart has forgotten to beat,
Till the hot blood has ceas'd to riot?

In Exeter Hall the saint may chide,
 The sinner may scoff outright,
The Bacchanal steep'd in the flagon's tide,
 Or the sensual Sybarite;
But NOLAN'S name will flourish in fame,
 When our galloping days are past,
When we go to the place from whence we came,
 Perchance to find rest at last.

Thy riddles grow dark, oh! drifting cloud,
 And thy misty shapes grow drear,
Thou hang'st in the air like a shadowy shroud,
 But I am of lighter cheer;
Though our future lot is a sable blot,
 Though the wise ones of earth will blame us,
Though our saddles will rot, and our rides be forgot,
 "DUM VIVIMUS, VIVAMUS!"

Fytte VIII
Finis Exoptatus
[A Metaphysical Song]

"There's something in this world amiss
Shall be unriddled by-and-bye." — Tennyson.

Boot and saddle, see, the slanting
 Rays begin to fall,
Flinging lights and colours flaunting
 Through the shadows tall.
Onward! onward! must we travel?
 When will come the goal?
Riddle I may not unravel,
 Cease to vex my soul.

Harshly break those peals of laughter

From the jays aloft,
Can we guess what they cry after?
 We have heard them oft;
Perhaps some strain of rude thanksgiving
 Mingles in their song,
Are they glad that they are living?
 Are they right or wrong?
Right, 'tis joy that makes them call so,
 Why should they be sad?
Certes! we are living also,
 Shall not we be glad?
Onward! onward! must we travel?
 Is the goal more near?
Riddle we may not unravel,
 Why so dark and drear?

Yon small bird his hymn outpouring,
 On the branch close by,
Recks not for the kestrel soaring
 In the nether sky,
Though the hawk with wings extended
 Poises over head,
Motionless as though suspended
 By a viewless thread.
See, he stoops, nay, shooting forward
 With the arrow's flight,
Swift and straight away to nor'ward
 Sails he out of sight.
Onward! onward! thus we travel,
 Comes the goal more nigh?
Riddle we may not unravel,
 Who shall make reply?

Ha! Friend Ephraim, saint or sinner,
 Tell me if you can —
Tho' we may not judge the inner,
 By the outer man,
Yet by girth of broadcloth ample,
 And by cheeks that shine,
Surely you set no example
 In the fasting line —

Could you, like yon bird, discov'ring,

Fate as close at hand,
As the kestrel o'er him hov'ring,
 Still, as he did, stand?
Trusting grandly, singing gaily,
 Confident and calm,
Not one false note in your daily
 Hymn or weekly psalm?

Oft your oily tones are heard in
 Chapel, where you preach,
This the everlasting burden
 Of the tale you teach:
"We are d— —d, our sins are deadly,
 You alone are heal'd" —
'Twas not thus their gospel redly
 Saints and martyrs seal'd.
You had seem'd more like a martyr,
 Than you seem to us,
To the beasts that caught a Tartar
 Once at Ephesus;
Rather than the stout apostle
 Of the Gentiles, who,
Pagan-like, could cuff and wrestle,
 They'd have chosen you.

Yet, I ween, on such occasion,
 Your dissenting voice
Would have been, in mild persuasion,
 Raised against their choice;
Man of peace, and man of merit,
 Pompous, wise, and grave,
Ephraim! is it flesh or spirit
 You strive most to save?
Vain is half this care and caution
 O'er the earthly shell,
We can neither baffle nor shun
 Dark plumed Azrael.
Onward! onward! still we wander,
 Nearer draws the goal;
Half the riddle's read, we ponder
 Vainly on the whole.

Eastward! in the pink horizon,

Fleecy hillocks shame
This dim range dull earth that lies on,
 Tinged with rosy flame.
Westward! as a stricken giant
 Stoops his bloody crest,
And tho' vanquished, frowns defiant,
 Sinks the sun to rest.
Distant, yet approaching quickly,
 From the shades that lurk,
Like a black pall gathers thickly,
 Night, when none may work.
Soon our restless occupation
 Shall have ceas'd to be;
Units! in God's vast creation,
 Ciphers! what are we?
Onward! onward! oh! faint-hearted;
 Nearer and more near
Has the goal drawn since we started,
 Be of better cheer.

Preacher! all forbearance ask, for
 All are worthless found,
Man must aye take man to task for
 Faults while earth goes round.
On this dank soil thistles muster,
 Thorns are broadcast sown;
Seek not figs where thistles cluster,
 Grapes where thorns have grown.

Sun and rain and dew from heaven,
 Light and shade and air,
Heat and moisture freely given,
 Thorns and thistles share.
Vegetation rank and rotten
 Feels the cheering ray;
Not uncared for, unforgotten,
 We, too, have our day.

Unforgotten! though we cumber
 Earth we work His will.
Shall we sleep through night's long slumber
 Unforgotten still?
Onward! onward! toiling ever,

Weary steps and slow,
Doubting oft, despairing never,
To the goal we go!

Hark! the bells on distant cattle
  Waft across the range;
Through the golden-tufted wattle,
  Music low and strange;
Like the marriage peal of fairies
  Comes the tinkling sound,
Or like chimes of sweet St. Mary's
  On far English ground.
How my courser champs the snaffle,
  And with nostril spread,
Snorts and scarcely seems to ruffle
  Fern leaves with his tread;
Cool and pleasant on his haunches
  Blows the evening breeze,
Through the overhanging branches
  Of the wattle trees:
Onward! to the Southern Ocean,
  Glides the breath of Spring.
Onward! with a dreary motion,
  I, too, glide and sing —
Forward! forward! still we wander —
  Tinted hills that lie
In the red horizon yonder —
  Is the goal so nigh?

Whisper, spring-wind, softly singing,
  Whisper in my ear;
Respite and nepenthe bringing,
  Can the goal be near?
Laden with the dew of vespers,
  From the fragrant sky,
In my ear the wind that whispers
  Seems to make reply —

"Question not, but live and labour
  Till yon goal be won,
Helping every feeble neighbour,
  Seeking help from none;
Life is mostly froth and bubble,

Two things stand like stone,
KINDNESS in another's trouble,
COURAGE in your own."

Courage, comrades, this is certain,
 All is for the best —
There are lights behind the curtain —
 Gentiles, let us rest.
As the smoke-rack veers to seaward,
 From "the ancient clay",
With its moral drifting leeward,
 Ends the wanderer's lay.

Borrow'd Plumes
[A Preface and a Piracy]

Prologue

Of borrow'd plumes I take the sin,
  My extracts will apply
To some few silly songs which in
  These pages scatter'd lie.

The words are Edgar Allan Poe's,
  As any man may see,
But what a POE-t wrote in prose,
  Shall make blank verse for me.

These trifles are collected and republished chiefly with a view to their redemption from the many improvements to which they have been subjected while going at random the rounds of the Press. I am naturally anxious that what I have written should circulate as I wrote it, if it circulate at all. * * * * * * In defence of my own taste, nevertheless, it is incumbent upon me to say that I think nothing in this volume of much value to the public, or very creditable to myself E. A. P.
       (See Preface to Poe's Poetical Works.)

Epilogue

And now that my theft stands detected,
  The first of my extracts may call
To some of the rhymes here collected
  Your notice, the second to all.

Ah! friend, you may shake your head sadly,
  Yet this much you'll say for my verse,
I've written of old something badly,
  But written anew something worse.

Pastor Cum
[Translation from Horace]

When he, that shepherd false, 'neath Phrygian sails,
  Carried his hostess Helen o'er the seas,
In fitful slumber Nereus hush'd the gales,
  That he might sing their future destinies.
A curse to your ancestral home you take
  With her, whom Greece, with many a soldier bold
Shall seek again, in concert sworn to break
  Your nuptial ties and Priam's kingdom old.
Alas! what sweat from man and horse must flow,
  What devastation to the Trojan realm
You carry, even now doth Pallas show
  Her wrath, preparing buckler, car, and helm.
In vain, secure in Aphrodite's care,
  You comb your locks, and on the girlish lyre
Select the strains most pleasant to the fair;
  In vain, on couch reclining, you desire
To shun the darts that threaten, and the thrust
  Of Cretan lance, the battle's wild turmoil,
And Ajax swift to follow — in the dust
  Condemned, though late, your wanton curls to soil.
Ah! see you not where (fatal to your race)
  Laertes' son comes with the Pylean sage;
Fearless alike, with Teucer joins the chase
  Stenelaus, skill'd the fistic strife to wage,
Nor less expert the fiery steeds to quell;
  And Meriones, you must know. Behold
A warrior, than his sire more fierce and fell,
  To find you rages, — Diomed the bold,
Whom like the stag that, far across the vale,
  The wolf being seen, no herbage can allure,
So fly you, panting sorely, dastard pale! —
  Not thus you boasted to your paramour.
Achilles' anger for a space defers
  The day of wrath to Troy and Trojan dame;
Inevitable glide the allotted years,
  And Dardan roofs must waste in Argive flame.

A Legend of Madrid
[Translated from the Spanish]

    Francesca.

Crush'd and throng'd are all the places
In our amphitheatre,
'Midst a sea of swarming faces
I can yet distinguish her;
Dost thou triumph, dark-brow'd Nina?
Is my secret known to thee?
On the sands of yon arena
I shall yet my vengeance see.
Now through portals fast careering
Picadors are disappearing;
Now the barriers nimbly clearing
Has the hindmost chulo flown.
Clots of dusky crimson streaking,
Brindled flanks and haunches reeking,
Wheels the wild bull, vengeance seeking,
On the matador alone.
Features by sombrero shaded,
Pale and passionless and cold;
Doublet richly laced and braided,
Trunks of velvet slash'd with gold,
Blood-red scarf, and bare Toledo, —
Mask more subtle, and disguise
Far less shallow, thou dost need, oh,
Traitor, to deceive my eyes.
Shouts of noisy acclamation,
Breathing savage expectation,
Greet him while he takes his station
Leisurely, disdaining haste;
Now he doffs his tall sombrero,
Fools! applaud your butcher hero,
Ye would idolise a Nero,
Pandering to public taste.

From the restless Guadalquivir
 To my sire's estates he came,
Woo'd and won me, how I shiver!
 Though my temples burn with shame.
I, a proud and high-born lady,
 Daughter of an ancient race,
'Neath the vine and olive shade I
 Yielded to a churl's embrace.
To a churl my vows were plighted,
Well my madness he requited,
Since, by priestly ties, united
 To the muleteer's child;
And my prayers are wafted o'er him,
That the bull may crush and gore him,
Since the love that once I bore him
 Has been changed to hatred wild.

   Nina.

Save him! aid him! oh, Madonna!
 Two are slain if he is slain;
Shield his life, and guard his honour,
 Let me not entreat in vain.
Sullenly the brindled savage
 Tears and tosses up the sand;
Horns that rend and hoofs that ravage,
 How shall man your shock withstand?
On the shaggy neck and head lie
Frothy flakes, the eyeballs redly
Flash, the horns so sharp and deadly
 Lower, short, and strong, and straight;
Fast, and furious, and fearless,
Now he charges; — virgin peerless,
Lifting lids, all dry and tearless,
 At thy throne I supplicate.

   Francesca.

Cool and calm, the perjured varlet
 Stands on strongly-planted heel,
In his left a strip of scarlet,

In his right a streak of steel;
Ah! the monster topples over,
 Till his haunches strike the plain! —
Low-born clown and lying lover,
 Thou hast conquer'd once again.

   Nina.

Sweet Madonna, maiden mother,
Thou hast saved him, and no other;
Now the tears I cannot smother,
 Tears of joy my vision blind;
Where thou sittest I am gazing,
These glad, misty eyes upraising,
I have pray'd, and I am praising,
 Bless thee! bless thee! virgin kind.

   Francesca.

While the crowd still sways and surges,
 Ere the applauding shouts have ceas'd,
See, the second bull emerges —
 'Tis the famed Cordovan beast, —
By the picador ungoaded,
 Scathless of the chulo's dart.
Slay him, and with guerdon loaded,
 And with honours crown'd depart.
No vain brutish strife he wages,
Never uselessly he rages,
And his cunning, as he ages,
 With his hatred seems to grow;
Though he stands amid the cheering,
Sluggish to the eye appearing,
Few will venture on the spearing
 Of so resolute a foe.

   Nina.

Courage, there is little danger,
 Yonder dull-eyed craven seems

Fitter far for stall and manger
 Than for scarf and blade that gleams;
Shorter, and of frame less massive,
 Than his comrade lying low,
Tame, and cowardly, and passive, —
 He will prove a feebler foe.
I have done with doubt and anguish,
Fears like dews in sunshine languish,
Courage, husband, we shall vanquish,
 Thou art calm and so am I.
For the rush he has not waited,
On he strides with step elated,
And the steel with blood unsated,
 Leaps to end the butchery.

   Francesca.

Tyro! mark the brands of battle
 On those shoulders dusk and dun,
Such as he is are the cattle
 Skill'd tauridors gladly shun;
Warier than the Andalusian,
 Swifter far, though not so large,
Think'st thou, to his own confusion,
 He, like him, will blindly charge?
Inch by inch the brute advances,
Stealthy yet vindictive glances,
Horns as straight as levell'd lances,
 Crouching withers, stooping haunches; —
Closer yet, until the tightening
Strains of rapt excitement height'ning
Grows oppressive. Ha! like lightning
 On his enemy he launches.

   Nina.

O'er the horn'd front drops the streamer,
 In the nape the sharp steel hisses,
Glances, grazes, — Christ! Redeemer!
 By a hair the spine he misses.

Francesca.

Hark! that shock like muffled thunder,
  Booming from the Pyrenees!
Both are down — the man is under —
  Now he struggles to his knees,
Now he sinks, his features leaden
Sharpen rigidly and deaden,
Sands beneath him soak and redden,
  Skies above him spin and veer;
Through the doublet torn and riven,
Where the stunted horn was driven,
Wells the life-blood — We are even,
  Daughter of the muleteer!

Fauconshawe
[A Ballad]

To fetch clear water out of the spring
 The little maid Margaret ran;
From the stream to the castle's western wing
 It was but a bowshot span;
On the sedgy brink where the osiers cling
 Lay a dead man, pallid and wan.

The lady Mabel rose from her bed,
 And walked in the castle hall,
Where the porch through the western turret led
 She met with her handmaid small.
"What aileth thee, Margaret?" the lady said,
 "Hast let thy pitcher fall?

"Say, what hast thou seen by the streamlet side —
 A nymph or a water sprite —
That thou comest with eyes so wild and wide,
 And with cheeks so ghostly white?"
"Nor nymph nor sprite," the maiden cried,
 "But the corpse of a slaughtered knight."

The lady Mabel summon'd straight
 To her presence Sir Hugh de Vere,
Of the guests who tarried within the gate
 Of Fauconshawe most dear
Was he to that lady; betrothed in state
 They had been since many a year.

"Little Margaret sayeth a dead man lies
 By the western spring, Sir Hugh;
I can scarce believe that the maiden lies —
 Yet scarce can believe her true."
And the knight replies, "Till we test her eyes
 Let her words gain credence due."

Down the rocky path knight and lady led,
  While guests and retainers bold
Followed in haste, for like wildfire spread
  The news by the maiden told.
They found 'twas even as she had said —
  The corpse had some while been cold.

How the spirit had pass'd in the moments last
  There was little trace to reveal:
On the still calm face lay no imprint ghast,
  Save the angel's solemn seal,
Yet the hands were clench'd in a death-grip fast,
  And the sods stamp'd down by the heel.

Sir Hugh by the side of the dead man knelt,
  Said, "Full well these features I know,
We have faced each other where blows were dealt,
  And he was a stalwart foe;
I had rather have met him hilt to hilt
  Than have found him lying low."

He turn'd the body up on its face,
  And never a word was spoken,
While he ripp'd the doublet, and tore the lace,
  And tugg'd — by the self-same token, —
And strain'd, till he wrench'd it out of its place,
  The dagger-blade that was broken.

Then he turned the body over again,
  And said, while he rose upright,
"May the brand of Cain, with its withering stain,
  On the murderer's forehead light,
For he never was slain on the open plain,
  Nor yet in the open fight."

Solemn and stern were the words he spoke,
  And he look'd at his lady's men,
But his speech no answering echoes woke,
  All were silent there and then,
Till a clear, cold voice the silence broke: —
  Lady Mabel cried, "Amen."

His glance met hers, the twain stood hush'd,

With the dead between them there;
But the blood to her snowy temples rush'd
  Till it tinged the roots of her hair,
Then paled, but a thin red streak still flush'd
  In the midst of her forehead fair.

Four yeomen raised the corpse from the ground,
  At a sign from Sir Hugh de Vere;
It was borne to the western turret round,
  And laid on a knightly bier,
With never a sob nor a mourning sound, —
  No friend to the dead was near.

Yet that night was neither revel nor dance
  In the halls of Fauconshawe;
Men looked askance with a doubtful glance
  At Sir Hugh, for they stood in awe
Of his prowess, but he, like one in a trance,
  Regarded naught that he saw.

* * * * *

Night black and chill, wind gathering still,
  With its wail in the turret tall,
And its headlong blast like a catapult cast
  On the crest of the outer wall,
And its hail and rain on the crashing pane,
  Till the glassy splinters fall.

A moody knight by the fitful light
  Of the great hall fire below;
A corpse upstairs, and a woman at prayers,
  Will they profit her, aye or no?
By'r lady fain, an' she comfort gain,
  There is comfort for us also.

The guests were gone, save Sir Hugh alone,
  And he watched the gleams that broke
On the pale hearth-stone, and flickered and shone
  On the panels of polish'd oak;
He was 'ware of no presence except his own
  Till the voice of young Margaret spoke:

"I've risen, Sir Hugh, at the mirk midnight,
 I cannot sleep in my bed,
Now, unless my tale can be told aright,
 I wot it were best unsaid;
It lies, the blood of yon northern knight,
 On my lady's hand and head."

"Oh! the wild wind raves and rushes along,
 But thy ravings seem more wild —
She never could do so foul a wrong —
 Yet I blame thee not, my child,
For the fever'd dreams on thy rest that throng!"
 He frown'd though his speech was mild.

"Let storm winds eddy, and scream, and hurl
 Their wrath, they disturb me naught;
The daughter she of a high-born earl,
 No secret of hers I've sought;
I am but the child of a peasant churl,
 Yet look to the proofs I've brought;

"This dagger snapp'd so close to the hilt —
 Dost remember thy token well?
Will it match with the broken blade that spilt
 His life in the western dell?
Nay! read her handwriting an' thou wilt,
 From her paramour's breast it fell."

The knight in silence the letter read,
 Oh! the characters well he knew!
And his face might have match'd the face of the dead,
 So ashen white was its hue!
Then he tore the parchment shred by shred,
 And the strips in the flames he threw.

And he muttered, "Densely those shadows fall
 In the copse where the alders thicken;
There she bade him come to her, once for all —
 Now, I well may shudder and sicken; —
Gramercy! that hand so white and small,
 How strongly it must have stricken."

* * * * *

At midnight hour, in the western tower,
  Alone with the dead man there,
Lady Mabel kneels, nor heeds nor feels
  The shock of the rushing air,
Though the gusts that pass through the riven glass
  Have scattered her raven hair.

Across the floor, through the opening door,
  Where standeth a stately knight,
The lamplight streams, and flickers, and gleams,
  On his features stern and white —
'Tis Sir Hugh de Vere, and he cometh more near,
  And the lady standeth upright.

"'Tis little," he said, "that I know or care
  Of the guilt (if guilt there be)
That lies 'twixt thee and yon dead man there,
  Nor matters it now to me;
I thought thee pure, thou art only fair,
  And to-morrow I cross the sea.

"He perish'd! I ask not why or how?
  I come to recall my troth;
Take back, my lady, thy broken vow,
  Give back my allegiance oath;
Let the past be buried between us now
  For ever — 'tis best for both.

"Yet, Mabel, I could ask, dost thou dare
  Lay hand on that corpse's heart,
And call on thy Maker, and boldly swear,
  That thou hadst in his death no part?
I ask not, while threescore proofs I share
  With one doubt — uncondemn'd thou art."

Oh! cold and bleak upon Mabel's cheek
  Came the blast of the storm-wind keen,
And her tresses black, as the glossy back
  Of the raven, glanced between
Her fingers slight, like the ivory white,
  As she parted their sable sheen.

Yet with steady lip, and with fearless eye,

And with cheek like the flush of dawn,
Unflinchingly she spoke in reply —
"Go hence with the break of morn,
I will neither confess, nor yet deny,
I will return thee scorn for scorn."

The knight bow'd low as he turn'd to go;
 He travell'd by land and sea,
But naught of his future fate I know,
 And naught of his fair ladye;
My story is told as, long ago,
 My story was told to me.

Rippling Water

The maiden sat by the river side
 (The rippling water murmurs by),
And sadly into the clear blue tide
 The salt tear fell from her clear blue eye.
"'Tis fixed for better, for worse," she cried,
"And to-morrow the bridegroom claims the bride.
Oh! wealth and power and rank and pride
 Can surely peace and happiness buy.
I was merry, nathless, in my girlhood's hours,
 'Mid the waving grass when the bright sun shone,
Shall I be as merry in Marmaduke's towers?"
 (The rippling water murmurs on).

Stephen works for his daily bread
 (The rippling water murmurs low).
Through the crazy thatch that covers his head
 The rain-drops fall and the wind-gusts blow.
"I'll mend the old roof-tree," so he said,
"And repair the cottage when we are wed."
And my pulses throbb'd, and my cheek grew red,
 When he kiss'd me — that was long ago.
Stephen and I, should we meet again,
 Not as we've met in days that are gone,
Will my pulses throb with pleasure or pain?
 (The rippling water murmurs on).

Old Giles, the gardener, strok'd my curls
 (The rippling water murmurs past),
Quoth he, "In laces and silks and pearls
 My child will see her reflection cast;
Now I trust in my heart that your lord will be
Kinder to you than he was to me,
When I lay in the gaol, and my children three,
 With their sickly mother, kept bitter fast."
With Marmaduke now my will is law,
 Marmaduke's will may be law anon;

Does the sheath of velvet cover the claw?
(The rippling water murmurs on).

Dame Martha patted me on the cheek
 (The rippling water murmurs low),
Saying, "There are words that I fain would speak —
 Perhaps they were best unspoken though;
I can't persuade you to change your mind,
And useless warnings are scarcely kind,
And I may be foolish as well as blind,
 But take my blessing whether or no."
Dame Martha's wise, though her hair is white,
 Her sense is good, though her sight is gone —
Can she really be gifted with second sight?
 (The rippling water murmurs on).

Brian of Hawksmede came to our cot
 (The rippling water murmurs by),
Scatter'd the sods of our garden plot,
 Riding his roan horse recklessly;
Trinket and token and tress of hair,
He flung them down at the door-step there,
Said, "Elsie! ask your lord, if you dare,
 Who gave him the blow as well as the lie."
That evening I mentioned Brian's name,
 And Marmaduke's face grew white and wan,
Am I pledged to one of a spirit so tame?
 (The rippling water murmurs on).

Brian is headstrong, rash, and vain
 (The rippling water murmurs still),
Stephen is somewhat duller of brain,
 Slower of speech, and milder of will;
Stephen must toil a living to gain,
Plough and harrow and gather the grain;
Brian has little enough to maintain
 The station in life which he needs must fill;
Both are fearless and kind and frank,
 But we can't win all gifts under the sun —
What have I won save riches and rank?
 (The rippling water murmurs on).

Riches and rank, and what beside?

(The rippling water murmurs yet),
The mansion is stately, the manor is wide,
 Their lord for a while may pamper and pet;
Liveried lackeys may jeer aside,
Though the peasant girl is their master's bride,
At her shyness, mingled with awkward pride, —
 'Twere folly for trifles like these to fret;
But the love of one that I cannot love,
 Will it last when the gloss of his toy is gone?
Is there naught beyond, below, or above?
 (The rippling water murmurs on).

Cui Bono

Oh! wind that whistles o'er thorns and thistles,
  Of this fruitful earth like a goblin elf;
Why should he labour to help his neighbour
  Who feels too reckless to help himself?
The wail of the breeze in the bending trees
  Is something between a laugh and a groan;
And the hollow roar of the surf on the shore
  Is a dull, discordant monotone;
I wish I could guess what sense they express,
  There's a meaning, doubtless, in every sound,
Yet no one can tell, and it may be as well —
  Whom would it profit? — The world goes round!

On this earth so rough we know quite enough,
  And, I sometimes fancy, a little too much;
The sage may be wiser than clown or than kaiser,
  Is he more to be envied for being such?
Neither more nor less, in his idleness
  The sage is doom'd to vexation sure;
The kaiser may rule, but the slippery stool,
  That he calls his throne, is no sinecure;
And as for the clown, you may give him a crown,
  Maybe he'll thank you, and maybe not,
And before you can wink he may spend it in drink —
  To whom does it profit? — We ripe and rot!

Yet under the sun much work is done
  By clown and kaiser, by serf and sage;
All sow and some reap, and few gather the heap
  Of the garner'd grain of a by-gone age.
By sea or by soil man is bound to toil,
  And the dreamer, waiting for time and tide,
For awhile may shirk his share of the work,
  But he grows with his dream dissatisfied;
He may climb to the edge of the beetling ledge,
  Where the loose crag topples and well-nigh reels

'Neath the lashing gale, but the tonic will fail —
What does it profit? — Wheels within wheels!

Aye! work we must, or with idlers rust,
 And eat we must our bodies to nurse;
Some folk grow fatter — what does it matter?
 I'm blest if I do — quite the reverse;
'Tis a weary round to which we are bound,
 The same thing over and over again;
Much toil and trouble, and a glittering bubble,
 That rises and bursts, is the best we gain;
And we murmur, and yet 'tis certain we get
 What good we deserve — can we hope for more? —
They are roaring, those waves, in their echoing caves —
 To whom do they profit? — Let them roar!

Bellona

Thou art moulded in marble impassive,
  False goddess, fair statue of strife,
Yet standest on pedestal massive,
  A symbol and token of life.
Thou art still, not with stillness of languor,
  And calm, not with calm boding rest;
For thine is all wrath and all anger
  That throbs far and near in the breast
    Of man, by thy presence possess'd.

With the brow of a fallen archangel,
  The lips of a beautiful fiend,
And locks that are snake-like to strangle,
  And eyes from whose depths may be glean'd
The presence of passions, that tremble
  Unbidden, yet shine as they may
Through features too proud to dissemble,
  Too cold and too calm to betray
    Their secrets to creatures of clay.

Thy breath stirreth faction and party,
  Men rise, and no voice can avail
To stay them — rose-tinted Astarte
  Herself at thy presence turns pale.
For deeper and richer the crimson
  That gathers behind thee throws forth
A halo thy raiment and limbs on,
  And leaves a red track in the path
    That flows from thy wine-press of wrath.

For behind thee red rivulets trickle,
  Men fall by thy hands swift and lithe,
As corn falleth down to the sickle,
  As grass falleth down to the scythe,
Thine arm, strong and cruel, and shapely,
  Lifts high the sharp, pitiless lance,

And rapine and ruin and rape lie
  Around thee. The Furies advance,
And Ares awakes from his trance.

We, too, with our bodies thus weakly,
  With hearts hard and dangerous, thus
We owe thee — the saints suffered meekly
  Their wrongs — it is not so with us.
Some share of thy strength thou hast given
  To mortals refusing in vain
Thine aid. We have suffered and striven
  Till we have grown reckless of pain,
Though feeble of heart and of brain.

Fair spirit, alluring if wicked,
  False deity, terribly real,
Our senses are trapp'd, our souls tricked
  By thee and thy hollow ideal.
The soldier who falls in his harness,
  And strikes his last stroke with slack hand,
On his dead face thy wrath and thy scorn is
  Imprinted. Oh! seeks he a land
Where he shall escape thy command?

When the blood of thy victims lies red on
  That stricken field, fiercest and last,
In the sunset that gilds Armageddon
  With battle-drift still overcast —
When the smoke of thy hot conflagrations
  O'ershadows the earth as with wings,
Where nations have fought against nations,
  And kings have encounter'd with kings,
When cometh the end of all things —

Then those who have patiently waited,
  And borne, unresisting, the pain
Of thy vengeance unglutted, unsated,
  Shall they be rewarded again?
Then those who, enticed by thy laurels,
  Or urged by thy promptings unblest,
Have striven and stricken in quarrels,
  Shall they, too, find pardon and rest?
We know not, yet hope for the best.

The Song of the Surf

White steeds of ocean, that leap with a hollow and wearisome roar
On the bar of ironstone steep, not a fathom's length from the shore,
Is there never a seer nor sophist can interpret your wild refrain,
When speech the harshest and roughest is seldom studied in vain?
My ears are constantly smitten by that dreary monotone,
In a hieroglyphic 'tis written — 'tis spoken in a tongue unknown;
Gathering, growing, and swelling, and surging, and shivering, say!
What is the tale you are telling? What is the drift of your lay?

You come, and your crests are hoary with the foam of your countless years;
You break, with a rainbow of glory, through the spray of your glittering tears.
Is your song a song of gladness? a paean of joyous might?
Or a wail of discordant sadness for the wrongs you never can right?
For the empty seat by the ingle? for children 'reft of their sire?
For the bride sitting sad, and single, and pale, by the flickering fire?
For your ravenous pools of suction? for your shattering billow swell?
For your ceaseless work of destruction? for your hunger insatiable?

Not far from this very place, on the sand and the shingle dry,
He lay, with his batter'd face upturned to the frowning sky.
When your waters wash'd and swill'd high over his drowning head,
When his nostrils and lungs were filled,
  when his feet and hands were as lead,
When against the rock he was hurl'd, and suck'd again to the sea,
On the shores of another world, on the brink of eternity,
On the verge of annihilation, did it come to that swimmer strong,
The sudden interpretation of your mystical, weird-like song?

"Mortal! that which thou askest, ask not thou of the waves;
Fool! thou foolishly taskest us — we are only slaves;
Might, more mighty, impels us — we must our lot fulfil,
He who gathers and swells us curbs us, too, at His will.
Think'st thou the wave that shatters questioneth His decree?
Little to us it matters, and naught it matters to thee.

Not thus, murmuring idly, we from our duty would swerve,
Over the world spread widely ever we labour and serve."

Whisperings in Wattle-Boughs

Oh, gaily sings the bird! and the wattle-boughs are stirr'd
 And rustled by the scented breath of spring;
Oh, the dreary wistful longing! Oh, the faces that are thronging!
 Oh, the voices that are vaguely whispering!

Oh, tell me, father mine, ere the good ship cross'd the brine,
 On the gangway one mute hand-grip we exchang'd;
Do you, past the grave, employ, for your stubborn, reckless boy,
 Those petitions that in life were ne'er estranged?

Oh, tell me, sister dear, parting word and parting tear
 Never pass'd between us; — let me bear the blame,
Are you living, girl, or dead? bitter tears since then I've shed
 For the lips that lisp'd with mine a mother's name.

Oh, tell me, ancient friend, ever ready to defend,
 In our boyhood, at the base of life's long hill,
Are you waking yet or sleeping? have you left this vale of weeping?
 Or do you, like your comrade, linger still?

Oh, whisper, buried love, is there rest and peace above? —
 There is little hope or comfort here below;
On your sweet face lies the mould, and your bed is straight and cold —
 Near the harbour where the sea-tides ebb and flow.

 *   *   *   *   *

All silent — they are dumb — and the breezes go and come
 With an apathy that mocks at man's distress;
Laugh, scoffer, while you may! I could bow me down and pray
 For an answer that might stay my bitterness.

Oh, harshly screams the bird! and the wattle-bloom is stirr'd;
 There's a sullen, weird-like whisper in the bough:
"Aye, kneel, and pray, and weep, but HIS BELOVED SLEEP
CAN NEVER BE DISTURB'D BY SUCH AS THOU!!"

Confiteor

The shore-boat lies in the morning light,
 By the good ship ready for sailing;
The skies are clear, and the dawn is bright,
Tho' the bar of the bay is fleck'd with white,
 And the wind is fitfully wailing;
Near the tiller stands the priest, and the knight
 Leans over the quarter-railing.

"There is time while the vessel tarries still,
 There is time while her shrouds are slack,
There is time ere her sails to the west wind fill,
Ere her tall masts vanish from town and from hill,
 Ere cleaves to her keel the track:
There is time for confession to those who will,
 To those who may never come back."

"Sir priest, you can shrive these men of mine,
 And, I pray you, shrive them fast,
And shrive those hardy sons of the brine,
Captain and mates of the EGLANTINE,
 And sailors before the mast;
Then pledge me a cup of the Cyprus wine,
 For I fain would bury the past."

"And hast thou naught to repent, my son?
 Dost thou scorn confession and shrift?
Ere thy sands from the glass of time shall run
Is there naught undone that thou should'st have done,
 Naught done that thou should'st have left?
The guiltiest soul may from guilt be won,
 And the stoniest heart may be cleft."

"Have my ears been closed to the prayer of the poor,
 Or deaf to the cry of distress?
Have I given little, and taken more?
Have I brought a curse to the widow's door?

Have I wrong'd the fatherless?
Have I steep'd my fingers in guiltless gore,
  That I must perforce confess?"

"Have thy steps been guided by purity
  Through the paths with wickedness rife?
Hast thou never smitten thine enemy?
Hast thou yielded naught to the lust of the eye,
  And naught to the pride of life?
Hast thou pass'd all snares of pleasure by?
  Hast thou shunn'd all wrath and strife?"

"Nay, certes! a sinful life I've led,
  Yet I've suffered, and lived in hope;
I may suffer still, but my hope has fled, —
I've nothing now to hope or to dread,
  And with fate I can fairly cope;
Were the waters closing over my head,
  I should scarcely catch at a rope."

"Dost suffer? thy pain may be fraught with grace,
  Since never by works alone
We are saved; — the penitent thief may trace
The wealth of love in the Saviour's face
  To the Pharisee rarely shown;
And the Magdalene's arms may yet embrace
  The foot of the jasper throne."

"Sir priest, a heavier doom I dree,
  For I feel no quickening pain,
But a dull, dumb weight when I bow my knee,
And (not with the words of the Pharisee)
  My hard eyes heavenward strain,
Where my dead darling prayeth for me!
  Now, I wot, she prayeth in vain!

"Still I hear it over the battle's din,
  And over the festive cheer, —
So she pray'd with clasp'd hands, white and thin, —
The prayer of a soul absolved from sin,
  For a soul that is dark and drear,
For the light of repentance bursting in,
  And the flood of the blinding tear.

"Say, priest! when the saint must vainly plead,
　Oh! how shall the sinner fare?
I hold your comfort a broken reed;
Let the wither'd branch for itself take heed,
　While the green shoots wait your care;
I've striven, though feebly, to grasp your creed,
　And I've grappled my own despair."

"By the little within thee, good and brave,
　Not wholly shattered, though shaken;
By the soul that crieth beyond the grave,
The love that He once in His mercy gave,
　In His mercy since retaken,
I conjure thee, oh! sinner, pardon crave,
　I implore thee, oh! sleeper, waken!"

"Go to! shall I lay my black soul bare
　To a vain, self-righteous man?
In my sin, in my sorrow, you may not share,
And yet could I meet with one who must bear
　The load of an equal ban,
With him I might strive to blend one prayer,
　The wail of the Publican."

"My son, I, too, am a withered bough,
　My place is to others given;
Thou hast sinn'd, thou sayest; I ask not how,
For I, too, have sinn'd, even as thou,
　And I, too, have feebly striven,
And with thee I must bow, crying, 'Shrive us now!
Our Father which art in heaven!'"

Sunlight on the Sea
[The Philosophy of a Feast]

Make merry, comrades, eat and drink
 (The sunlight flickers on the sea),
The garlands gleam, the glasses clink,
 The grape juice mantles fair and free,
The lamps are trimm'd, although the light
 Of day still lingers on the sky;
We sit between the day and night,
 And push the wine flask merrily.
I see you feasting round me still,
 All gay of heart and strong of limb;
Make merry, friends, your glasses fill,
 The lights are growing dim.

I miss the voice of one I've heard
 (The sunlight sinks upon the sea),
He sang as blythe as any bird,
 And shook the rafters with his glee;
But times have changed with him, I wot,
 By fickle fortune cross'd and flung;
Far stouter heart than mine he's got
 If now he sings as then he sung.
Yet some must swim when others sink,
 And some must sink when others swim;
Make merry, comrades, eat and drink,
 The lights are growing dim.

I miss the face of one I've loved
 (The sunlight settles on the sea) —
Long since to distant climes he roved,
 He had his faults, and so have we;
His name was mentioned here this day,
 And it was coupled with a sneer;
I heard, nor had I aught to say,
 Though once I held his memory dear.
Who cares, 'mid wines and fruits and flowers,

Though death or danger compass him;
He had his faults, and we have ours,
  The lights are growing dim.

I miss the form of one I know
  (The sunlight wanes upon the sea) —
'Tis not so very long ago,
  We drank his health with three-times-three,
And we were gay when he was here;
  And he is gone, and we are gay.
Where has he gone? or far or near?
  Good sooth, 'twere somewhat hard to say.
You glance aside, you doubtless think
  My homily a foolish whim,
'Twill soon be ended, eat and drink,
  The lights are growing dim.

The fruit is ripe, the wine is red
  (The sunlight fades upon the sea);
To us the absent are the dead,
  The dead to us must absent be.
We, too, the absent ranks must join;
  And friends will censure and forget:
There's metal base in every coin;
  Men vanish, leaving traces yet
Of evil and of good behind,
  Since false notes taint the skylark's hymn,
And dross still lurks in gold refined —
  The lights are growing dim.

We eat and drink or e'er we die
  (The sunlight flushes on the sea).
Three hundred soldiers feasted high
  An hour before Thermopylae;
Leonidas pour'd out the wine,
  And shouted ere he drain'd the cup,
"Ho! comrades, let us gaily dine —
  This night with Pluto we shall sup";
And if they leant upon a reed,
  And if their reed was slight and slim,
There's something good in Spartan creed —
  The lights are growing dim.

Make merry, comrades, eat and drink
 (The sunlight flashes on the sea);
My spirit is rejoiced to think
 That even as they were so are we;
For they, like us, were mortals vain,
 The slaves to earthly passions wild,
Who slept with heaps of Persians slain
 For winding-sheets around them piled.
The dead man's deeds are living still —
 My Festive speech is somewhat grim —
Their good obliterates their ill —
 The lights are growing dim.

We eat and drink, we come and go
 (The sunlight dies upon the open sea).
I speak in riddles. Is it so?
 My riddles need not mar your glee;
For I will neither bid you share
 My thoughts, nor will I bid you shun,
Though I should see in yonder chair
 Th' Egyptian's muffled skeleton.
One toast with me your glasses fill,
 Aye, fill them level with the brim,
De mortuis, nisi bonum, nil!
 The lights are growing dim.

Delilah
[From a Picture]

The sun has gone down, spreading wide on
 The sky-line one ray of red fire;
Prepare the soft cushions of Sidon,
 Make ready the rich loom of Tyre.
The day, with its toil and its sorrow,
 Its shade, and its sunshine, at length
Has ended; dost fear for the morrow,
 Strong man, in the pride of thy strength?

Like fire-flies, heavenward clinging,
 They multiply, star upon star;
And the breeze a low murmur is bringing
 From the tents of my people afar.
Nay, frown not, I am but a Pagan,
 Yet little for these things I care;
'Tis the hymn to our deity Dagon
 That comes with the pleasant night air.

It shall not disturb thee, nor can it;
 See, closed are the curtains, the lights
Gleam down on the cloven pomegranate,
 Whose thirst-slaking nectar invites;
The red wine of Hebron glows brightly
 In yon goblet — the draught of a king;
And through the silk awning steals lightly
 The sweet song my handmaidens sing.

Dost think that thy God, in His anger,
 Will trifle with nature's great laws,
And slacken those sinews in languor
 That battled so well in His cause?
Will He take back that strength He has given,
 Because to the pleasures of youth
Thou yieldest? Nay, Godlike, in heaven,
 He laughs at such follies, forsooth.

Oh! were I, for good or for evil,
 As great and as gifted as thou,
Neither God should restrain me, nor devil,
 To none like a slave would I bow.
If fate must indeed overtake thee,
 And feebleness come to thy clay,
Pause not till thy strength shall forsake thee,
 Enjoy it the more in thy day.

Oh, fork'd-tongue of adder, by her pent
 In smooth lips! — oh, Sybarite blind!
Oh, woman allied to the serpent!
 Oh, beauty with venom combined!
Oh, might overcoming the mighty!
 Oh, glory departing! oh, shame!
Oh, altar of false Aphrodite,
 What strength is consumed in thy flame!

Strong chest, where her drapery rustles,
 Strong limbs by her black tresses hid!
Not alone by the might of your muscles
 Yon lion was rent like a kid!
The valour from virtue that sunders,
 Is 'reft of its nobler part;
And Lancelot's arm may work wonders,
 But braver is Galahad's heart.

Sleep sound on that breast fair and ample;
 Dull brain, and dim eyes, and deaf ears,
Feel not the cold touch on your temple,
 Heed not the faint clash of the shears.
It comes! — with the gleam of the lamps on
 The curtains — that voice — does it jar
On thy soul in the night-watch? Ho! Samson,
 Upon thee the Philistines are.

From Lightning and Tempest

The spring-wind pass'd through the forest, and whispered low in the leaves,
 And the cedar toss'd her head, and the oak stood firm in his pride;
The spring-wind pass'd through the town,
  through the housetops, casements, and eaves,
 And whisper'd low in the hearts of the men, and the men replied,
Singing — "Let us rejoice in the light
Of our glory, and beauty, and might;
 Let us follow our own devices, and foster our own desires.
As firm as our oaks in our pride, as our cedars fair in our sight,
 We stand like the trees of the forest
   that brave the frosts and the fires."

The storm went forth to the forest, the plague went forth to the town,
 And the men fell down to the plague, as the trees fell down to the gale;
And their bloom was a ghastly pallor, and their smile was a ghastly frown,
 And the song of their hearts was changed to a wild, disconsolate wail,
Crying — "God! we have sinn'd, we have sinn'd,
We are bruis'd, we are shorn, we are thinn'd,
 Our strength is turn'd to derision, our pride laid low in the dust,
Our cedars are cleft by Thy lightnings, our oaks are strew'd by Thy wind,
 And we fall on our faces seeking Thine aid, though Thy wrath is just."

Wormwood and Nightshade

The troubles of life are many,
 The pleasures of life are few;
When we sat in the sunlight, Annie,
 I dreamt that the skies were blue —
When we sat in the sunlight, Annie,
 I dreamt that the earth was green;
There is little colour, if any,
 'Neath the sunlight now to be seen.

Then the rays of the sunset glinted
 Through the blackwoods' emerald bough
On an emerald sward, rose-tinted,
 And spangled, and gemm'd; — and now
The rays of the sunset redden
 With a sullen and lurid frown,
From the skies that are dark and leaden,
 To earth that is dusk and brown.

To right and to left extended
 The uplands are blank and drear,
And their neutral tints are blended
 With the dead leaves sombre and sere;
The cold grey mist from the still side
 Of the lake creeps sluggish and sure,
Bare and bleak is the hill-side,
 Barren and bleak the moor.

Bright hues and shapes intertwisted,
 Fair forms and rich colours; — now
They have flown — if e'er they existed —
 It matters not why or how.
It matters not where or when, dear,
 They have flown, the blue and the green,
I thought on what might be then, dear,
 Now I think on what might have been.

What might have been! — words of folly;
　What might be! — speech for a fool;
With mistletoe round me, and holly,
　Scarlet and green, at Yule.
With the elm in the place of the wattle,
　And in lieu of the gum, the oak,
Years back I believed a little,
　And as I believed I spoke.

Have I done with those childish fancies?
　They suited the days gone by,
When I pulled the poppies and pansies,
　When I hunted the butterfly,
With one who has long been sleeping,
　A stranger to doubts and cares,
And to sowing that ends in reaping
　Thistles, and thorns, and tares.

What might be! — the dreams were scatter'd,
　As chaff is toss'd by the wind,
The faith has been rudely shattered
　That listen'd with credence blind;
Things were to have been, and therefore
　They were, and they are to be,
And will be; — we must prepare for
　The doom we are bound to dree.

Ah, me! we believe in evil,
　Where once we believed in good,
The world, the flesh, and the devil
　Are easily understood;
The world, the flesh, and the devil
　Their traces on earth are plain;
Must they always riot and revel
　While footprints of man remain?

Talk about better and wiser,
　Wiser and worse are one,
The sophist is the despiser
　Of all things under the sun;
Is nothing real but confusion?
　Is nothing certain but death?
Is nothing fair save illusion?

Is nothing good that has breath?

Some sprite, malignant and elfish,
 Seems present whispering close,
"All motives of life are selfish,
 All instincts of life are gross;
And the song that the poet fashions,
 And the love-bird's musical strain,
Are jumbles of animal passions,
 Refined by animal pain."

The restless throbbings and burnings
 That hope unsatisfied brings,
The weary longings and yearnings
 For the mystical better things,
Are the sands on which is reflected
 The pitiless moving lake,
Where the wanderer falls dejected,
 By a thirst he never can slake.

A child blows bubbles that glitter,
 He snatches them, they disperse;
Yet childhood's folly is better,
 And manhood's folly is worse;
Gilt baubles we grasp at blindly
 Would turn in our hands to dross;
'Tis a fate less cruel than kindly
 Denies the gain and the loss.

And as one who pursues a shadow,
 As one who hunts in a dream,
As the child who crosses the meadow,
 Enticed by the rainbow's gleam,
I — knowing the course was foolish,
 And guessing the goal was pain,
Stupid, and stubborn, and mulish —
 Followed and follow again.

The sun over Gideon halted,
 Holding aloof the night,
When Joshua's arm was exalted,
 Yet never retraced his flight;
Nor will he turn back, nor can he,

He chases the future fast;
The future is blank — oh, Annie!
I fain would recall the past.

There are others toiling and straining
  'Neath burdens graver than mine —
They are weary, yet uncomplaining —
  I know it, yet I repine;
I know it, how time will ravage,
  How time will level, and yet
I long with a longing savage,
  I regret with a fierce regret.

You are no false ideal,
  Something is left of you,
Present, perceptible, real,
  Palpable, tangible, true;
One shred of your broken necklace,
  One tress of your pale, gold hair,
And a heart so utterly reckless,
  That the worst it would gladly dare.

There is little pleasure, if any,
  In waking the past anew;
My days and nights have been many;
  Lost chances many I rue —
My days and nights have been many;
  Now I pray that they be few,
When I think on the hill-side, Annie,
  Where I dreamt that the skies were blue.

Ars Longa
[A Song of Pilgrimage]

Our hopes are wild imaginings,
 Our schemes are airy castles,
Yet these, on earth, are lords and kings,
 And we their slaves and vassals;
Your dream, forsooth, of buoyant youth,
 Most ready to deceive is;
But age will own the bitter truth,
 "Ars longa, vita brevis."

The hill of life with eager feet
 We climbed in merry morning,
But on the downward track we meet
 The shades of twilight warning;
The shadows gaunt they fall aslant,
 And those who scaled Ben Nevis,
Against the mole-hills toil and pant,
 "Ars longa, vita brevis."

The obstacles that barr'd our path
 We seldom quail'd to dash on
In youth, for youth one motto hath,
 "The will, the way must fashion."
Those words, I wot, blood thick and hot,
 Too ready to believe is,
But thin and cold our blood hath got,
 "Ars longa, vita brevis."

And "art is long", and "life is short",
 And man is slow at learning;
And yet by divers dealings taught,
 For divers follies yearning,
He owns at last, with grief downcast
 (For man disposed to grieve is) —
One adage old stands true and fast,
 "Ars longa, vita brevis."
We journey, manhood, youth, and age,

The matron, and the maiden,
Like pilgrims on a pilgrimage,
 Loins girded, heavy laden: —
Each pilgrim strong, who joins our throng,
 Most eager to achieve is,
Foredoom'd ere long to swell the song,
 "Ars longa, vita brevis."

At morn, with staff and sandal-shoon,
 We travel brisk and cheery,
But some have laid them down ere noon,
 And all at eve are weary;
The noontide glows with no repose,
 And bitter chill the eve is,
The grasshopper a burden grows,
 "Ars longa, vita brevis."

The staff is snapp'd, the sandal fray'd,
 The flint-stone galls and blisters,
Our brother's steps we cannot aid,
 Ah me! nor aid our sister's:
The pit prepares its hidden snares,
 The rock prepared to cleave is,
We cry, in falling unawares,
 "Ars longa, vita brevis."

Oh! Wisdom, which we sought to win!
 Oh! Strength, in which we trusted!
Oh! Glory, which we gloried in!
 Oh! puppets we adjusted!
On barren land our seed is sand,
 And torn the web we weave is,
The bruised reed hath pierced the hand,
 "Ars longa, vita brevis."

We, too, "Job's comforters" have met,
 With steps, like ours, unsteady,
They could not help themselves, and yet
 To judge us they were ready;
Life's path is trod at last, and God
 More ready to reprieve is,
They know who rest beneath the sod,
 "Mors gratum, vita brevis."

The Last Leap

All is over! fleet career,
 Dash of greyhound slipping thongs,
Flight of falcon, bound of deer,
Mad hoof-thunder in our rear,
 Cold air rushing up our lungs,
 Din of many tongues.

Once again, one struggle good,
 One vain effort; — he must dwell
Near the shifted post, that stood
Where the splinters of the wood,
 Lying in the torn tracks, tell
 How he struck and fell.

Crest where cold drops beaded cling,
 Small ear drooping, nostril full,
Glazing to a scarlet ring,
Flanks and haunches quivering,
 Sinews stiff'ning, void and null,
 Dumb eyes sorrowful.

Satin coat that seems to shine
 Duller now, black braided tress,
That a softer hand than mine
Far away was wont to twine,
 That in meadows far from this
 Softer lips might kiss.

All is over! this is death,
 And I stand to watch thee die,
Brave old horse! with 'bated breath
Hardly drawn through tight-clenched teeth,
 Lip indented deep, but eye
 Only dull and dry.

Musing on the husk and chaff

Gather'd where life's tares are sown,
Thus I speak, and force a laugh
That is half a sneer and half
An involuntary groan,
In a stifled tone —

"Rest, old friend! thy day, though rife
With its toil, hath ended soon;
We have had our share of strife,
Tumblers in the mask of life,
In the pantomime of noon
Clown and pantaloon.

"With the flash that ends thy pain
Respite and oblivion blest
Come to greet thee. I in vain
Fall: I rise to fall again:
Thou hast fallen to thy rest —
And thy fall is best!"

Quare Fatigasti

Two years ago I was thinking
 On the changes that years bring forth;
Now I stand where I then stood drinking
 The gust and the salt sea froth;
And the shuddering wave strikes, linking
With the waves subsiding and sinking,
And clots the coast herbage, shrinking,
 With the hue of the white cere-cloth.

Is there aught worth losing or keeping?
 The bitters or sweets men quaff?
The sowing or the doubtful reaping?
 The harvest of grain or chaff?
Or squandering days or heaping,
Or waking seasons or sleeping,
The laughter that dries the weeping,
 Or the weeping that drowns the laugh?

For joys wax dim and woes deaden,
 We forget the sorrowful biers,
And the garlands glad that have fled in
 The merciful march of years;
And the sunny skies, and the leaden,
And the faces that pale or redden,
And the smiles that lovers are wed in
 Who are born and buried in tears.

And the myrtle bloom turns hoary,
 And the blush of the rose decays,
And sodden with sweat and gory
 Are the hard won laurels and bays;
We are neither joyous nor sorry
When time has ended our story,
And blotted out grief and glory,
 And pain, and pleasure, and praise.

Weigh justly, throw good and bad in
 The scales, will the balance veer
With the joys or the sorrows had in
 The sum of a life's career?
In the end, spite of dreams that sadden
The sad or the sanguine madden,
There is nothing to grieve or gladden,
 There is nothing to hope or fear.

"Thou hast gone astray," quoth the preacher,
 "In the gall of thy bitterness,"
Thou hast taught me in vain, oh, teacher!
 I neither blame thee nor bless;
If bitter is sure and sweet sure,
These vanish with form and feature —
Can the creature fathom the creature,
 Whose Creator is fathomless?

Is this dry land sure? Is the sea sure?
 Is there aught that shall long remain,
Pain, or peril, or pleasure,
 Pleasure, or peril, or pain?
Shall we labour or take our leisure,
And who shall inherit treasure,
If the measure with which we measure
 Is meted to us again?

I am slow in learning and swift in
 Forgetting, and I have grown
So weary with long sand sifting;
 T'wards the mist where the breakers moan
The rudderless bark is drifting,
Through the shoals and the quicksands shifting —
In the end shall the night-rack lifting,
 Discover the shores unknown?

Hippodromania; or, Whiffs from the Pipe

In Five Parts

Part I
Visions in the Smoke

Rest, and be thankful! On the verge
 Of the tall cliff rugged and grey,
But whose granite base the breakers surge,
 And shiver their frothy spray,
Outstretched, I gaze on the eddying wreath
 That gathers and flits away,
With the surf beneath, and between my teeth
 The stem of the "ancient clay".

With the anodyne cloud on my listless eyes,
 With its spell on my dreamy brain,
As I watch the circling vapours rise
From the brown bowl up to the sullen skies,
 My vision becomes more plain,
Till a dim kaleidoscope succeeds
 Through the smoke-rack drifting and veering,
Like ghostly riders on phantom steeds
 To a shadowy goal careering.

In their own generation the wise may sneer,
 They hold our sports in derision;
Perchance to sophist, or sage, or seer,
 Were allotted a graver vision.
Yet if man, of all the Creator plann'd,
 His noblest work is reckoned,
Of the works of His hand, by sea or by land,
 The horse may at least rank second.

Did they quail, those steeds of the squadrons light,

Did they flinch from the battle's roar,
When they burst on the guns of the Muscovite,
 By the echoing Black Sea shore?
On! on! to the cannon's mouth they stride,
 With never a swerve nor a shy,
Oh! the minutes of yonder maddening ride,
 Long years of pleasure outvie!

No slave, but a comrade staunch, in this,
 Is the horse, for he takes his share,
Not in peril alone, but in feverish bliss,
 And in longing to do and dare.
Where bullets whistle, and round shot whiz,
 Hoofs trample, and blades flash bare,
God send me an ending as fair as his
 Who died in his stirrups there!

The wind has slumbered throughout the day,
Now a fitful gust springs over the bay,
My wandering thoughts no longer stray,
 I'll fix my overcoat buttons;
Secure my old hat as best I may
(And a shocking bad one it is, by the way),
Blow a denser cloud from my stunted clay,
And then, friend BELL, as the Frenchmen say,
 We'll "go back again to our muttons".

There's a lull in the tumult on yonder hill,
 And the clamour has grown less loud,
Though the Babel of tongues is never still,
 With the presence of such a crowd.
The bell has rung. With their riders up
 At the starting post they muster,
The racers stripp'd for the "Melbourne Cup",
 All gloss and polish and lustre;
And the course is seen, with its emerald sheen,
 By the bright spring-tide renew'd,
Like a ribbon of green stretched out between
 The ranks of the multitude.

The flag is lowered. "They're off!" "They come!"
 The squadron is sweeping on;
A sway in the crowd — a murmuring hum:

"They're here!" "They're past!" "They're gone!"
They came with the rush of the southern surf,
 On the bar of the storm-girt bay;
And like muffled drums on the sounding turf
 Their hoof-strokes echo away.

The rose and black draws clear of the ruck,
 And the murmur swells to a roar,
As the brave old colours that never were struck,
 Are seen with the lead once more.
Though the feathery ferns and grasses wave
 O'er the sod where Lantern sleeps,
Though the turf is green on Fisherman's grave,
 The stable its prestige keeps.

Six lengths in front she scours along,
 She's bringing the field to trouble;
She's tailing them off, she's running strong,
 She shakes her head and pulls double.
Now Minstrel falters and Exile flags,
 The Barb finds the pace too hot,
And Toryboy loiters, and Playboy lags,
 And the BOLT of Ben Bolt is shot.

That she never may be caught this day,
 Is the worst that the public wish her.
She won't be caught: she comes right away;
 Hurrah for Seagull and Fisher!
See, Strop falls back, though his reins are slack,
 Sultana begins to tire,
And the top-weight tells on the Sydney crack,
 And the pace on "the Gippsland flyer".

The rowels, as round the turn they sweep,
 Just graze Tim Whiffler's flanks;
Like the hunted deer that flies through the sheep,
 He strides through the beaten ranks.
Daughter of Omen, prove your birth,
 The colt will take lots of choking;
The hot breath steams at your saddle girth,
 From his scarlet nostril smoking.

The shouts of the Ring for a space subside,

And slackens the bookmaker's roar;
Now, Davis, rally; now, Carter, ride,
　As man never rode before.
When Sparrowhawk's backers cease to cheer,
　When Yattendon's friends are dumb,
When hushed is the clamour for Volunteer —
　Alone in the race they come!

They're neck and neck; they're head and head;
　They're stroke for stroke in the running;
The whalebone whistles, the steel is red,
　No shirking as yet nor shunning.
One effort, Seagull, the blood you boast
　Should struggle when nerves are strained; —
With a rush on the post, by a neck at the most,
　The verdict for Tim is gained.

Tim Whiffler wins. Is blood alone
　The sine qua non for a flyer?
The breed of his dam is a myth unknown,
　And we've doubts respecting his sire.
Yet few (if any) those proud names are,
　On the pages of peerage or stud,
In whose 'scutcheon lurks no sinister bar,
　No taint of the base black blood.

Aye, Shorthouse, laugh — laugh loud and long,
　For pedigree you're a sticker;
You may be right, I may be wrong,
　Wiseacres both! Let's liquor.
Our common descent we may each recall
　To a lady of old caught tripping,
The fair one in fig leaves, who d— —d us all
　For a bite at a golden pippin.

When first on this rocky ledge I lay,
There was scarce a ripple in yonder bay,
　The air was serenely still;
Each column that sailed from my swarthy clay
Hung loitering long ere it passed away,
Though the skies wore a tinge of leaden grey,
　And the atmosphere was chill.
But the red sun sank to his evening shroud,

Where the western billows are roll'd,
Behind a curtain of sable cloud,
 With a fringe of scarlet and gold;
There's a misty glare in the yellow moon,
 And the drift is scudding fast,
There'll be storm, and rattle, and tempest soon,
 When the heavens are overcast.
The neutral tint of the sullen sea
 Is fleck'd with the snowy foam,
And the distant gale sighs drearilie,
 As the wanderer sighs for his home.
The white sea-horses toss their manes
 On the bar of the southern reef,
And the breakers moan, and — by Jove, it rains
 (I thought I should come to grief);
Though it can't well damage my shabby hat,
 Though my coat looks best when it's damp;
Since the shaking I got (no matter where at),
 I've a mortal dread of the cramp.
My matches are wet, my pipe's put out,
 And the wind blows colder and stronger;
I'll be stiff, and sore, and sorry, no doubt,
 If I lie here any longer.

Part II
The Fields of Coleraine

On the fields of Col'raine there'll be labour in vain
 Before the Great Western is ended,
The nags will have toil'd, and the silks will be soil'd,
 And the rails will require to be mended.

For the gullies are deep, and the uplands are steep,
 And mud will of purls be the token,
And the tough stringy-bark, that invites us to lark,
 With impunity may not be broken.

Though Ballarat's fast, and they say he can last,

And that may be granted hereafter,
Yet the judge's decision to the Border division
  Will bring neither shouting nor laughter.

And Blueskin, I've heard that he goes like a bird,
  And I'm told that to back him would pay me;
He's a good bit of stuff, but not quite good enough,
  "Non licuit credere famae."

Alfred ought to be there, we all of us swear
  By the blood of King Alfred, his sire;
He's not the real jam, by the blood of his dam,
  So I sha'n't put him down as a flyer.

Now, Hynam, my boy, I wish you great joy,
  I know that when fresh you can jump, sir;
But you'll scarce be in clover, when you're ridden all over,
  And punished from shoulder to rump, sir.

Archer goes like a shot, they can put on their pot,
  And boil it to cover expenses;
Their pot will boil over, the run of his dover
  He'll never earn over big fences.

There's a horse in the race, with a blaze on his face,
  And we know he can gallop a docker!
He's proved himself stout, of his speed there's no doubt,
  And his jumping's according to Cocker.

When Hynam's outstripp'd, and when Alfred is whipp'd,
  To keep him in sight of the leaders,
While Blueskin runs true, but his backers look blue,
  For his rider's at work with the bleeders;

When his carcase of beef brings "the bullock" to grief,
  And the rush of the tartan is ended;
When Archer's in trouble — who's that pulling double,
  And taking his leaps unextended?

He wins all the way, and the rest — sweet, they say,
  Is the smell of the newly-turned plough, friend,
But you smell it too close when it stops eyes and nose,
  And you can't tell your horse from your cow, friend.

Part III
Credat Judaeus Apella

Dear Bell, — I enclose what you ask in a letter,
 A short rhyme at random, no more and no less,
And you may insert it, for want of a better,
 Or leave it, it doesn't much matter, I guess;
And as for a tip, why, there isn't much in it,
 I may hit the right nail, but first, I declare,
I haven't a notion what's going to win it
 (The Champion, I mean), and what's more, I don't care.
Imprimis, there's Cowra — few nags can go quicker
 Than she can — and Smith takes his oath she can fly;
While Brown, Jones, and Robinson swear she's a sticker,
 But "credat Judaeus Apella", say I.

There's old Volunteer, I'd be sorry to sneer
 At his chance; he'll be there, if he goes at the rate
He went at last year, when a customer queer,
 Johnny Higgerson, fancied him lock'd in the straight;
I've heard that the old horse has never been fitter,
 I've heard all performances past he'll outvie;
He may gallop a docker, and finish a splitter,
 But "credat Judaeus Apella", say I.

I know what they say, sir, "The Hook" he can stay, sir,
 And stick to his work like a sleuth-hound or beagle;
He stays "with a HOOK", and he sticks in the clay, sir;
 I'd rather, for choice, pop my money on Seagull;
I'm told that the Sydney division will rue, sir,
 Their rashness in front of the stand when they spy,
With a clear lead, the white jacket spotted with blue, sir,
 But "credat Judaeus Apella", say I.

There's The Barb — you may talk of your flyers and stayers,
 All bosh — when he strips you can see his eye range
Round his rivals, with much the same look as Tom Sayers
 Once wore when he faced the big novice, Bill Bainge.
Like Stow, at our hustings, confronting the hisses
 Of roughs, with his queer Mephistopheles' smile;
Like Baker, or Baker's more wonderful MRS.,

The terror of blacks at the source of the Nile;
Like Triton 'mid minnows; like hawk among chickens;
 Like — anything better than everything else:
He stands at the post. Now they're off! the plot thickens!
 Quoth Stanley to Davis, "How is your pulse?"
He skims o'er the smooth turf, he scuds through the mire,
 He waits with them, passes them, bids them good-bye!
Two miles and three-quarters, cries Filgate, "He'll tire."
 Oh! "credat Judaeus Apella", say I.

Lest my tale should come true, let me give you fair warning,
 You may "shout" some cheroots, if you like, no champagne
For this child — "Oh! think of my head in the morning,"
 Old chap, you don't get me on that lay again.
The last time those games I look'd likely to try on,
 Says Bradshawe, "You'll feel very sheepish and shy
When you are haul'd up and caution'd by D——g——y and L——n,"
 Oh! "credat Judaeus Apella", say I.

This writing bad verses is very fatiguing,
 The brain and the liver against it combine,
And nerves with digestion in concert are leaguing,
 To punish excess in the pen and ink line;
Already I feel just as if I'd been rowing
 Hard all — on a supper of onions and tripe
(A thing I abhor), but my steam I've done blowing,
 I am, my dear BELL, yours truly, "The Pipe".

P.S. — Tell J. P., if he fancies a good 'un,
 That old chestnut pony of mine is for sale.
N.B. — His forelegs are uncommonly wooden,
 I fancy the near one's beginning to fail,
And why shouldn't I do as W——n does oft,
 And swear that a cripple is sound — on the Bible —
Hold hard! though the man I allude to is soft,
 He's game to go in for an action of libel.

Part IV
Banker's Dream

Of chases and courses dogs dream, so do horses —
  Last night I was dozing and dreaming,
The crowd and the bustle were there, and the rustle
  Of the silk in the autumn sky gleaming.

The stand throng'd with faces, the broadcloth and laces,
  The booths, and the tents, and the cars,
The bookmakers' jargon, for odds making bargain,
  The nasty stale smell of cigars.

We formed into line, 'neath the merry sunshine,
  Near the logs at the end of the railing;
"Are you ready, boys? Go!" cried the starter, and low
  Sank the flag, and away we went sailing.

In the van of the battle we heard the stones rattle,
  Some slogging was done, but no slaughter,
A shout from the stand, and the whole of our band
  Skimm'd merrily over the water.

Two fences we clear'd, and the roadway we near'd,
  When three of our troop came to trouble;
Like a bird on the wing, or a stone from a sling,
  Flew Cadger, first over the double.

And Western was there, head and tail in the air,
  And Pondon was there, too — what noodle
Could so name a horse? I should feel some remorse
  If I gave such a name to a poodle.

In and out of the lane, to the racecourse again,
  Craig's pony was first, I was third,
And Ingleside lit in my tracks, with the bit
  In his teeth, and came up "like a bird".

In the van of the battle we heard the rails rattle,
  Says he, "Though I don't care for shunning
My share of the raps, I shall look out for gaps,

When the light weight's away with the running."

At the fence just ahead the outsider still led,
  The chestnut play'd follow my leader;
Oh! the devil a gap, he went into it slap,
  And he and his jock took a header.

Says Ingleside, "Mate, should the pony go straight,
  You've no time to stop or turn restive;"
Says I, "Who means to stop? I shall go till I drop;"
  Says he, "Go it, old cuss, gay and festive."

The fence stiff and tall, just beyond the log wall,
  We cross'd, and the walls, and the water, —
I took off too near, a small made fence to clear,
  And just touch'd the grass with my snorter.

At the next post and rail up went Western's bang tail,
  And down (by the very same token)
To earth went his nose, for the panel he chose
  Stood firm and refused to be broken.

I dreamt someone said that the bay would have made
  The race safe if he'd STOOD a while longer;
IF he had, — but, like if, there the panel stands stiff —
  He stood, but the panel stood stronger.

In and out of the road, with a clear lead still show'd
  The violet fluted with amber;
Says Johnson, "Old man, catch him now if you can,
  'Tis the second time round you'll remember."

At the road once again, pulling hard on the rein,
  Craig's pony popp'd in and popp'd out;
I followed like smoke and the pace was no joke,
  For his friends were beginning to shout.

And Ingleside came to my side, strong and game,
  And once he appear'd to outstrip me,
But I felt the steel gore, and I shot to the fore,
  Only Cadger seem'd likely to whip me.

In the van of the battle I heard the logs rattle,

His stroke never seem'd to diminish,
And thrice I drew near him, and thrice he drew clear,
For the weight served him well at the finish.

Ha! Cadger goes down, see, he stands on his crown —
Those rails take a power of clouting —
A long sliding blunder — he's up — well, I wonder
If now it's all over but shouting.

All loosely he's striding, the amateur's riding
All loosely, some reverie locked in
Of a "vision in smoke", or a "wayfaring bloke",
His poetical rubbish concocting.

Now comes from afar the faint cry, "Here they are,"
"The violet winning with ease,"
"Fred goes up like a shot," "Does he catch him or not?"
Level money, I'll take the cerise.

To his haunches I spring, and my muzzle I bring
To his flank, to his girth, to his shoulder;
Through the shouting and yelling I hear my name swelling,
The hearts of my backers grow bolder.

Neck and neck! head and head! staring eye! nostril spread!
Girth and stifle laid close to the ground!
Stride for stride! stroke for stroke! through one hurdle we've broke!
On the splinters we've lit with one bound.

And "Banker for choice" is the cry, and one voice
Screams "Six to four once upon Banker;"
"Banker wins," "Banker's beat," "Cadger wins," "A dead heat" —
Ah! there goes Fred's whalebone a flanker.

Springs the whip with a crack! nine stone ten on his back,
Fit and light he can race like the devil;
I draw past him — 'tis vain; he draws past me again,
Springs the whip! and again we are level.

Steel and cord do their worst, now my head struggles first!
That tug my last spurt has expended —
Nose to nose! lip to lip! from the sound of the whip
He strains to the utmost extended.

How they swim through the air, as we roll to the chair,
 Stand, faces, and railings flit past;
Now I spring * * *
        from my lair with a snort and a stare,
Rous'd by Fred with my supper at last.

Part V
Ex Fumo Dare Lucem
['Twixt the Cup and the Lip]

Prologue

Calm and clear! the bright day is declining,
 The crystal expanse of the bay,
Like a shield of pure metal, lies shining
 'Twixt headlands of purple and grey,
While the little waves leap in the sunset,
 And strike with a miniature shock,
In sportive and infantine onset,
 The base of the iron-stone rock.

Calm and clear! the sea-breezes are laden
 With a fragrance, a freshness, a power,
With a song like the song of a maiden,
 With a scent like the scent of a flower;
And a whisper, half-weird, half-prophetic,
 Comes home with the sigh of the surf; —
But I pause, for your fancies poetic
 Never rise from the level of "Turf".

Fellow-bungler of mine, fellow-sinner,
 In public performances past,
In trials whence touts take their winner,
 In rumours that circulate fast,
In strains from Prunella or Priam,
 Staying stayers, or goers that go,
You're much better posted than I am,

'Tis little I care, less I know.

Alas! neither poet nor prophet
 Am I, though a jingler of rhymes —
'Tis a hobby of mine, and I'm off it
 At times, and I'm on it at times;
And whether I'm off it or on it,
 Your readers my counsels will shun,
Since I scarce know Van Tromp from Blue Bonnet,
 Though I might know Cigar from the Nun.

With "visions" you ought to be sated
 And sicken'd by this time, I swear
That mine are all myths self-created,
 Air visions that vanish in air;
If I had some loose coins I might chuck one,
 To settle this question and say,
"Here goes! this is tails for the black one,
 And heads for my fav'rite the bay."

And must I rob Paul to pay Peter,
 Or Peter defraud to pay Paul?
My rhymes, are they stale? if my metre
 Is varied, one chime rings through all:
One chime — though I sing more or sing less,
 I have but one string to my lute,
And it might have been better if, stringless
 And songless, the same had been mute.

Yet not as a seer of visions,
 Nor yet as a dreamer of dreams,
I send you these partial decisions
 On hackney'd, impoverish'd themes;
But with song out of tune, sung to pass time,
 Flung heedless to friends or to foes,
Where the false notes that ring for the last time,
 May blend with some real ones, who knows?

Poems of Adam Lindsay Gordon

The Race

On the hill they are crowding together,
 In the stand they are crushing for room,
Like midge-flies they swarm on the heather,
 They gather like bees on the broom;
They flutter like moths round a candle —
 Stale similes, granted, what then?
I've got a stale subject to handle,
 A very stale stump of a pen.

Hark! the shuffle of feet that are many,
 Of voices the many-tongued clang —
"Has he had a bad night?" "Has he any
 Friends left?" — How I hate your turf slang;
'Tis stale to begin with, not witty,
 But dull, and inclined to be coarse,
But bad men can't use (more's the pity)
 Good words when they slate a good horse.

Heu! heu! quantus equis (that's Latin
 For "bellows to mend" with the weeds),
They're off! lights and shades! silk and satin!
 A rainbow of riders and steeds!
And one shows in front, and another
 Goes up and is seen in his place,
Sic transit (more Latin) — Oh! bother,
 Let's get to the end of the race.

* * * * *

See, they come round the last turn careering,
 Already Tait's colours are struck,
And the green in the vanguard is steering,
 And the red's in the rear of the ruck!
Are the stripes in the shade doom'd to lie long?
 Do the blue stars on white skies wax dim?
Is it Tamworth or Smuggler? 'Tis Bylong
 That wins — either Bylong or Tim.

As the shell through the breach that is riven
 And sapp'd by the springing of mines,

As the bolt from the thunder-cloud driven,
  That levels the larches and pines,
Through yon mass parti-colour'd that dashes
  Goal-turn'd, clad in many-hued garb,
From rear to van, surges and flashes
  The yellow and black of The Barb.

Past The Fly, falling back on the right, and
  The Gull, giving way on the left,
Past Tamworth, who feels the whip smite, and
  Whose sides by the rowels are cleft;
Where Tim and the chestnut together
  Still bear of the battle the brunt,
As if eight stone twelve were a feather,
  He comes with a rush to the front.

Tim Whiffler may yet prove a Tartar,
  And Bylong's the horse that can stay,
But Kean is in trouble — and Carter
  Is hard on the satin-skinn'd bay;
And The Barb comes away unextended,
  Hard held, like a second Eclipse,
While behind the hoof-thunder is blended
  With the whistling and crackling of whips.

Epilogue

He wins; yes, he wins upon paper,
  He hasn't yet won upon turf,
And these rhymes are but moonshine and vapour,
  Air-bubbles and spume from the surf.
So be it, at least they are given
  Free, gratis, for just what they're worth,
And (whatever there may be in heaven)
  There's little worth much upon earth.

When, with satellites round them the centre,
  Of all eyes, hard press'd by the crowd,
The pair, horse and rider, re-enter
  The gate, 'mid a shout long and loud,
You may feel, as you might feel, just landed

Full length on the grass from the clip
Of a vicious cross-counter, right-handed,
Or upper-cut whizzing from hip.

And that's not so bad if you're pick'd up
 Discreetly, and carefully nursed;
Loose teeth by the sponge are soon lick'd up,
 And next time you MAY get home first.
Still I'm not sure you'd like it exactly
 (Such tastes as a rule are acquired),
And you'll find in a nutshell this fact lie,
 Bruised optics are not much admired.

Do I bore you with vulgar allusions?
 Forgive me, I speak as I feel,
I've pondered and made my conclusions —
 As the mill grinds the corn to the meal;
So man striving boldly but blindly,
 Ground piecemeal in Destiny's mill,
At his best, taking punishment kindly,
 Is only a chopping-block still.

Are we wise? Our abstruse calculations
 Are based on experience long;
Are we sanguine? Our high expectations
 Are founded on hope that is strong;
Thus we build an air-castle that crumbles
 And drifts till no traces remain,
And the fool builds again while he grumbles,
 And the wise one laughs, building again.

"How came they to pass, these rash blunders,
 These false steps so hard to defend?"
Our friend puts the question and wonders,
 We laugh and reply, "Ah! my friend,
Could you trace the first stride falsely taken,
 The distance misjudged, where or how,
When you pick'd yourself up, stunn'd and shaken,
 At the fence 'twixt the turf and the plough?"

In the jar of the panel rebounding!
 In the crash of the splintering wood!
In the ears to the earth shock resounding!

In the eyes flashing fire and blood!
In the quarters above you revolving!
 In the sods underneath heaving high!
There was little to aid you in solving
 Such questions — the how or the why.

And destiny, steadfast in trifles,
 Is steadfast for better or worse
In great things, it crushes and stifles,
 And swallows the hopes that we nurse.
Men wiser than we are may wonder,
 When the future they cling to so fast,
To the roll of that destiny's thunder,
 Goes down with the wrecks of the past.

* * * * *

The past! the dead past! that has swallow'd
 All the honey of life and the milk,
Brighter dreams than mere pastimes we've follow'd,
 Better things than our scarlet or silk;
Aye, and worse things — that past is it really
 Dead to us who again and again
Feel sharply, hear plainly, see clearly,
 Past days with their joy and their pain?

Like corpses embalm'd and unburied
 They lie, and in spite of our will,
Our souls on the wings of thought carried,
 Revisit their sepulchres still;
Down the channels of mystery gliding,
 They conjure strange tales, rarely read,
Of the priests of dead Pharaohs presiding
 At mystical feasts of the dead.

Weird pictures arise, quaint devices,
 Rude emblems, baked funeral meats,
Strong incense, rare wines, and rich spices,
 The ashes, the shrouds, and the sheets;
Does our thraldom fall short of completeness
 For the magic of a charnel-house charm,
And the flavour of a poisonous sweetness,
 And the odour of a poisonous balm?

And the links of the past — but, no matter,
 For I'm getting beyond you, I guess,
And you'll call me "as mad as a hatter"
 If my thoughts I too freely express;
I subjoin a quotation, pray learn it,
 And with the aid of your lexicon tell us
The meaning thereof — "Res discernit
 Sapiens, quas confundit asellus."

Already green hillocks are swelling,
 And combing white locks on the bar,
Where a dull, droning murmur is telling
 Of winds that have gather'd afar;
Thus we know not the day, nor the morrow,
 Nor yet what the night may bring forth,
Nor the storm, nor the sleep, nor the sorrow,
 Nor the strife, nor the rest, nor the wrath.

Yet the skies are still tranquil and starlit,
 The sun 'twixt the wave and the west
Dies in purple, and crimson, and scarlet,
 And gold; let us hope for the best,
Since again from the earth his effulgence
 The darkness and damp-dews shall wipe.
Kind reader, extend your indulgence
 To this the last lay of "The Pipe".

The Roll of the Kettledrum; or, The Lay of the Last Charger

"You have the Pyrrhic dance as yet,
 Where is the Pyrrhic phalanx gone?
Of two such lessons, why forget
 The nobler and the manlier one?" — Byron.

One line of swart profiles and bearded lips dressing,
 One ridge of bright helmets, one crest of fair plumes,
One streak of blue sword-blades all bared for the fleshing,
 One row of red nostrils that scent battle-fumes.

Forward! the trumpets were sounding the charge,
 The roll of the kettledrum rapidly ran,
That music, like wild-fire spreading at large,
 Madden'd the war-horse as well as the man.

Forward! still forward! we thunder'd along,
 Steadily yet, for our strength we were nursing;
Tall Ewart, our sergeant, was humming a song,
 Lance-corporal Black Will was blaspheming and cursing.

Open'd their volley of guns on our right,
 Puffs of grey smoke, veiling gleams of red flame,
Curling to leeward, were seen on the height,
 Where the batteries were posted, as onward we came.

Spreading before us their cavalry lay,
 Squadron on squadron, troop upon troop;
We were so few, and so many were they —
 Eagles wait calmly the sparrow-hawk's stoop.

Forward! still forward! steed answering steed
 Cheerily neigh'd, while the foam flakes were toss'd
From bridle to bridle — the top of our speed
 Was gain'd, but the pride of our order was lost.

One was there leading by nearly a rood,

Though we were racing he kept to the fore,
Still as a rock in his stirrups he stood,
High in the sunlight his sabre he bore.

Suddenly tottering, backwards he crash'd,
Loudly his helm right in front of us rung;
Iron hoofs thunder'd, and naked steel flash'd
Over him — youngest, where many were young.

Now we were close to them, every horse striding
Madly; — St. Luce pass'd with never a groan; —
Sadly my master look'd round — he was riding
On the boy's right, with a line of his own.

Thrusting his hand in his breast or breast-pocket,
While from his wrist the sword swung by a chain,
Swiftly he drew out some trinket or locket,
Kiss'd it (I think) and replaced it again.

Burst, while his fingers reclosed on the haft,
Jarring concussion and earth shaking din,
Horse 'counter'd horse, and I reel'd, but he laugh'd,
Down went his man, cloven clean to the chin!

Wedged in the midst of that struggling mass,
After the first shock, where each his foe singled,
Little was seen, save a dazzle, like glass
In the sun, with grey smoke and black dust intermingled.

Here and there redden'd a pistol shot, flashing
Through the red sparkle of steel upon steel!
Redder the spark seem'd, and louder the clashing,
Struck from the helm by the iron-shod heel!

Over fallen riders, like wither'd leaves strewing
Uplands in autumn, we sunder'd their ranks;
Steeds rearing and plunging, men hacking and hewing,
Fierce grinding of sword-blades, sharp goading of flanks.

Short was the crisis of conflict soon over,
Being too good (I suppose) to last long;
Through them we cut, as the scythe cuts the clover,
Batter'd and stain'd we emerg'd from their throng.

Some of our saddles were emptied, of course;
  To heaven (or elsewhere) Black Will had been carried!
Ned Sullivan mounted Will's riderless horse,
  His mare being hurt, while ten seconds we tarried.

And then we re-formed, and went at them once more,
  And ere they had rightly closed up the old track,
We broke through the lane we had open'd before,
  And as we went forward e'en so we came back.

Our numbers were few, and our loss far from small,
  They could fight, and, besides, they were twenty to one;
We were clear of them all when we heard the recall,
  And thus we returned, but my tale is not done.

For the hand of my rider felt strange on my bit,
  He breathed once or twice like one partially choked,
And sway'd in his seat, then I knew he was hit; —
  He must have bled fast, for my withers were soak'd,

And scarcely an inch of my housing was dry;
  I slacken'd my speed, yet I never quite stopp'd,
Ere he patted my neck, said, "Old fellow, good-bye!"
  And dropp'd off me gently, and lay where he dropp'd!

Ah, me! after all, they may call us dumb creatures —
  I tried hard to neigh, but the sobs took my breath,
Yet I guess'd gazing down at those still, quiet features,
  He was never more happy in life than in death.

* * * * *

Two years back, at Aldershot, Elrington mentioned
  My name to our colonel one field-day. He said,
"'Count', 'Steeltrap', and 'Challenger' ought to be pension'd;"
  "Count" died the same week, and now "Steeltrap" is dead.

That morning our colonel was riding "Theresa",
  The filly by "Teddington" out of "Mistake";
His girls, pretty Alice and fair-haired Louisa,
  Were there on the ponies he purchased from Blake.

I remember he pointed me out to his daughters,

Said he, "In this troop I may fairly take pride,
But I've none left like him in my officers' quarters,
 Whose life-blood the mane of old 'Challenger' dyed."

Where are they? the war-steeds who shared in our glory,
 The "Lanercost" colt, and the "Acrobat" mare,
And the Irish division, "Kate Kearney" and "Rory",
 And rushing "Roscommon", and eager "Kildare",

And "Freeny", a favourite once with my master,
 And "Warlock", a sluggard, but honest and true,
And "Tancred", as honest as "Warlock", but faster,
 And "Blacklock", and "Birdlime", and "Molly Carew"? —

All vanish'd, what wonder! twelve summers have pass'd
 Since then, and my comrade lies buried this day, —
Old "Steeltrap", the kicker, — and now I'm the last
 Of the chargers who shared in that glorious fray.

* * * * *

Come, "Harlequin", keep your nose out of my manger,
 You'll get your allowance, my boy, and no more;
Snort! "Silvertail", snort! when you've seen as much danger
 As I have, you won't mind the rats in the straw.

* * * * *

Our gallant old colonel came limping and halting,
 The day before yesterday, into my stall;
Oh! light to the saddle I've once seen him vaulting,
 In full marching order, steel broadsword and all.

And now his left leg than his right is made shorter
 Three inches, he stoops, and his chest is unsound;
He spoke to me gently, and patted my quarter,
 I laid my ears back, and look'd playfully round.

For that word kindly meant, that caress kindly given,
 I thank'd him, though dumb, but my cheerfulness fled;
More sadness I drew from the face of the living
 Than years back I did from the face of the dead.

For the dead face, upturn'd, tranquil, joyous, and fearless,
　Look'd straight from green sod to blue fathomless sky
With a smile; but the living face, gloomy and tearless,
　And haggard and harass'd, look'd down with a sigh.

Did he think on the first time he kiss'd Lady Mary?
　On the morning he wing'd Horace Greville the beau?
On the winner he steer'd in the grand military?
　On the charge that he headed twelve long years ago?

Did he think on each fresh year, of fresh grief the herald?
　On lids that are sunken, and locks that are grey?
On Alice, who bolted with Brian Fitzgerald?
　On Rupert, his first-born, dishonour'd by "play"?

On Louey, his darling, who sleeps 'neath the cypress,
　That shades her and one whose last breath gave her life?
I saw those strong fingers hard over each eye press —
　Oh! the dead rest in peace when the quick toil in strife!

　　* 　* 　* 　* 　*

Scoff, man! egotistical, proud, unobservant,
　Since I with man's grief dare to sympathise thus;
Why scoff? — fellow-creature I am, fellow-servant
　Of God, can man fathom God's dealings with us?

The wide gulf that parts us may yet be no wider
　Than that which parts you from some being more blest;
And there may be more links 'twixt the horse and his rider
　Than ever your shallow philosophy guess'd.

You are proud of your power, and vain of your courage,
　And your blood, Anglo-Saxon, or Norman, or Celt;
Though your gifts you extol, and our gifts you disparage,
　Your perils, your pleasures, your sorrows we've felt.

We, too, sprung from mares of the prophet of Mecca,
　And nursed on the pride that was born with the milk,
And filtered through "Crucifix", "Beeswing", "Rebecca",
　We love sheen of scarlet and shimmer of silk.

We, too, sprung from loins of the Ishmaelite stallions,

We glory in daring that dies or prevails;
From 'counter of squadrons, and crash of battalions,
  To rending of blackthorns, and rattle of rails.

In all strife where courage is tested, and power,
  From the meet on the hill-side, the horn-blast, the find,
The burst, the long gallop that seems to devour
  The champaign, all obstacles flinging behind,

To the cheer and the clarion, the war-music blended
  With war-cry, the furious dash at the foe,
The terrible shock, the recoil, and the splendid
  Bare sword, flashing blue, rising red from the blow.

I've borne ONE through perils where many have seen us,
  No tyrant, a kind friend, a patient instructor,
And I've felt some strange element flashing between us,
  Till the saddle seem'd turn'd to a lightning conductor.

Did he see? could he feel through the faintness, the numbness,
  While linger'd the spirit half-loosed from the clay,
Dumb eyes seeking his in their piteous dumbness,
  Dumb quivering nostrils, too stricken to neigh?

And what then? the colours reversed, the drums muffled,
  The black nodding plumes, the dead march and the pall,
The stern faces, soldier-like, silent, unruffled,
  The slow sacred music that floats over all!

Cross carbine and boar-spear, hang bugle and banner,
  Spur, sabre, and snaffle, and helm — Is it well?
Vain 'scutcheon, false trophies of Mars and Diana, —
  Can the dead laurel sprout with the live immortelle?

It may be, — we follow, and though we inherit
  Our strength for a season, our pride for a span,
Say! vanity are they? vexation of spirit?
  Not so, since they serve for a time horse and man.

They serve for a time, and they make life worth living,
  In spite of life's troubles — 'tis vain to despond;
Oh, man! WE at least, WE enjoy, with thanksgiving,
  God's gifts on this earth, though we look not beyond.

YOU sin, and YOU suffer, and we, too, find sorrow,
 Perchance through YOUR sin — yet it soon will be o'er;
We labour to-day, and we slumber to-morrow,
 Strong horse and bold rider! — and WHO KNOWETH MORE?

* * * * *

In our barrack-square shouted Drill-sergeant M'Cluskie,
 The roll of the kettledrum rapidly ran,
The colonel wheel'd short, speaking once, dry and husky,
 "Would to God I had died with your master, old man!"

[End of Sea Spray and Smoke Drift.]

Bush Ballads & Galloping Rhymes

A Dedication
to the Author of "Holmby House"

They are rhymes rudely strung with intent less
   Of sound than of words,
In lands where bright blossoms are scentless,
   And songless bright birds;
Where, with fire and fierce drought on her tresses,
Insatiable Summer oppresses
Sere woodlands and sad wildernesses,
   And faint flocks and herds.

Where in dreariest days, when all dews end,
   And all winds are warm,
Wild Winter's large flood-gates are loosen'd,
   And floods, freed by storm,
From broken up fountain heads, dash on
Dry deserts with long pent up passion —
Here rhyme was first framed without fashion,
   Song shaped without form.

Whence gather'd? — The locust's glad chirrup
   May furnish a stave;
The ring of a rowel and stirrup,
   The wash of a wave.
The chaunt of the marsh frog in rushes,
That chimes through the pauses and hushes
Of nightfall, the torrent that gushes,
   The tempests that rave.

In the deep'ning of dawn, when it dapples
   The dusk of the sky,
With streaks like the redd'ning of apples,
   The ripening of rye.

To eastward, when cluster by cluster,
Dim stars and dull planets that muster,
Wax wan in a world of white lustre
   That spreads far and high.

In the gathering of night gloom o'erhead, in
   The still silent change,
All fire-flushed when forest trees redden
   On slopes of the range.
When the gnarl'd, knotted trunks Eucalyptian
Seem carved, like weird columns Egyptian,
With curious device — quaint inscription,
   And hieroglyph strange.

In the Spring, when the wattle gold trembles
   'Twixt shadow and shine,
When each dew-laden air draught resembles
   A long draught of wine;
When the sky-line's blue burnish'd resistance
Makes deeper the dreamiest distance,
Some song in all hearts hath existence, —
   Such songs have been mine.

They came in all guises, some vivid
   To clasp and to keep;
Some sudden and swift as the livid
   Blue thunder-flame's leap.
This swept through the first breath of clover
With memories renew'd to the rover —
That flash'd while the black horse turn'd over
   Before the long sleep.

To you (having cunning to colour
   A page with your pen,
That through dull days, and nights even duller,
   Long years ago ten,
Fair pictures in fever afforded) —
I send these rude staves, roughly worded
By one in whose brain stands recorded
   As clear now as then,

"The great rush of grey 'Northern water',
   The green ridge of bank,

The 'sorrel' with curved sweep of quarter
   Curl'd close to clean flank,
The Royalist saddlefast squarely,
And where the bright uplands stretch fairly,
Behind, beyond pistol-shot barely,
   The Roundheaded rank.

"A long launch, with clinging of muscles,
   And clenching of teeth!
The loose doublet ripples and rustles!
   The swirl shoots beneath!"
Enough. In return for your garland —
In lieu of the flowers from your far land —
Take wild growth of dreamland or starland,
   Take weeds for your wreath.

Yet rhyme had not fail'd me for reason,
   Nor reason for rhyme,
Sweet Song! had I sought you in season,
   And found you in time.
You beckon in your bright beauty yonder,
And I, waxing fainter, yet fonder,
Now weary too soon when I wander —
   Now fall when I climb.

It matters but little in the long run,
   The weak have some right —
Some share in the race that the strong run,
   The fight the strong fight.
If words that are worthless go westward,
Yet the worst word shall be as the best word,
In the day when all riot sweeps restward,
   In darkness or light.

The Sick Stockrider

Hold hard, Ned! Lift me down once more, and lay me in the shade.
　Old man, you've had your work cut out to guide
Both horses, and to hold me in the saddle when I sway'd,
　All through the hot, slow, sleepy, silent ride.
The dawn at "Moorabinda" was a mist rack dull and dense,
　The sunrise was a sullen, sluggish lamp;
I was dozing in the gateway at Arbuthnot's bound'ry fence,
　I was dreaming on the Limestone cattle camp.
We crossed the creek at Carricksford, and sharply through the haze,
　And suddenly the sun shot flaming forth;
To southward lay "Katawa", with the sandpeaks all ablaze,
　And the flush'd fields of Glen Lomond lay to north.
Now westward winds the bridle path that leads to Lindisfarm,
　And yonder looms the double-headed Bluff;
From the far side of the first hill, when the skies are clear and calm,
　You can see Sylvester's woolshed fair enough.
Five miles we used to call it from our homestead to the place
　Where the big tree spans the roadway like an arch;
'Twas here we ran the dingo down that gave us such a chase
　Eight years ago — or was it nine? — last March.

'Twas merry in the glowing morn, among the gleaming grass,
　To wander as we've wandered many a mile,
And blow the cool tobacco cloud, and watch the white wreaths pass,
　Sitting loosely in the saddle all the while.
'Twas merry 'mid the blackwoods, when we spied the station roofs,
　To wheel the wild scrub cattle at the yard,
With a running fire of stockwhips and a fiery run of hoofs;
　Oh! the hardest day was never then too hard!

Aye! we had a glorious gallop after "Starlight" and his gang,
　When they bolted from Sylvester's on the flat;
How the sun-dried reed-beds crackled, how the flint-strewn ranges rang
　To the strokes of "Mountaineer" and "Acrobat".
Hard behind them in the timber, harder still across the heath,

Close beside them through the tea-tree scrub we dash'd;
And the golden-tinted fern leaves, how they rustled underneath!
And the honeysuckle osiers, how they crash'd!

We led the hunt throughout, Ned, on the chestnut and the grey,
　And the troopers were three hundred yards behind,
While we emptied our six-shooters on the bushrangers at bay,
　In the creek with stunted box-tree for a blind!
There you grappled with the leader, man to man and horse to horse,
　And you roll'd together when the chestnut rear'd;
He blazed away and missed you in that shallow watercourse —
　A narrow shave — his powder singed your beard!

In these hours when life is ebbing, how those days when life was young
　Come back to us; how clearly I recall
Even the yarns Jack Hall invented, and the songs Jem Roper sung;
　And where are now Jem Roper and Jack Hall?

Aye! nearly all our comrades of the old colonial school,
　Our ancient boon companions, Ned, are gone;
Hard livers for the most part, somewhat reckless as a rule,
　It seems that you and I are left alone.

There was Hughes, who got in trouble through that business with the cards,
　It matters little what became of him;
But a steer ripp'd up MacPherson in the Cooraminta yards,
　And Sullivan was drown'd at Sink-or-swim;
And Mostyn — poor Frank Mostyn — died at last a fearful wreck,
　In "the horrors", at the Upper Wandinong,
And Carisbrooke, the rider, at the Horsefall broke his neck,
　Faith! the wonder was he saved his neck so long!

Ah! those days and nights we squandered at the Logans' in the glen —
　The Logans, man and wife, have long been dead.
Elsie's tallest girl seems taller than your little Elsie then;
　And Ethel is a woman grown and wed.

I've had my share of pastime, and I've done my share of toil,
　And life is short — the longest life a span;
I care not now to tarry for the corn or for the oil,
　Or for the wine that maketh glad the heart of man.

For good undone and gifts misspent and resolutions vain,
  'Tis somewhat late to trouble. This I know —
I should live the same life over, if I had to live again;
  And the chances are I go where most men go.

The deep blue skies wax dusky, and the tall green trees grow dim,
  The sward beneath me seems to heave and fall;
And sickly, smoky shadows through the sleepy sunlight swim,
  And on the very sun's face weave their pall.
Let me slumber in the hollow where the wattle blossoms wave,
  With never stone or rail to fence my bed;
Should the sturdy station children pull the bush flowers on my grave,
  I may chance to hear them romping overhead.

The Swimmer

With short, sharp, violent lights made vivid,
 To southward far as the sight can roam,
Only the swirl of the surges livid,
 The seas that climb and the surfs that comb.
Only the crag and the cliff to nor'ward,
And the rocks receding, and reefs flung forward,
And waifs wreck'd seaward and wasted shoreward
 On shallows sheeted with flaming foam.

A grim, grey coast and a seaboard ghastly,
 And shores trod seldom by feet of men —
Where the batter'd hull and the broken mast lie,
 They have lain embedded these long years ten.
Love! when we wander'd here together,
Hand in hand through the sparkling weather,
From the heights and hollows of fern and heather,
 God surely loved us a little then.

The skies were fairer and shores were firmer —
 The blue sea over the bright sand roll'd;
Babble and prattle, and ripple and murmur,
 Sheen of silver and glamour of gold —
And the sunset bath'd in the gulf to lend her
A garland of pinks and of purples tender,
A tinge of the sun-god's rosy splendour,
 A tithe of his glories manifold.

Man's works are graven, cunning, and skilful
 On earth, where his tabernacles are;
But the sea is wanton, the sea is wilful,
 And who shall mend her and who shall mar?
Shall we carve success or record disaster
On the bosom of her heaving alabaster?
Will her purple pulse beat fainter or faster
 For fallen sparrow or fallen star?

I would that with sleepy, soft embraces
　The sea would fold me — would find me rest,
In luminous shades of her secret places,
　In depths where her marvels are manifest;
So the earth beneath her should not discover
My hidden couch — nor the heaven above her —
As a strong love shielding a weary lover,
　I would have her shield me with shining breast.

When light in the realms of space lay hidden,
　When life was yet in the womb of time,
Ere flesh was fettered to fruits forbidden,
　And souls were wedded to care and crime,
Was the course foreshaped for the future spirit —
A burden of folly, a void of merit —
That would fain the wisdom of stars inherit,
　And cannot fathom the seas sublime?

Under the sea or the soil (what matter?
　The sea and the soil are under the sun),
As in the former days in the latter,
　The sleeping or waking is known of none.
Surely the sleeper shall not awaken
To griefs forgotten or joys forsaken,
For the price of all things given and taken,
　The sum of all things done and undone.

Shall we count offences or coin excuses,
　Or weigh with scales the soul of a man,
Whom a strong hand binds and a sure hand looses,
　Whose light is a spark and his life a span?
The seed he sow'd or the soil he cumber'd,
The time he served or the space he slumber'd,
Will it profit a man when his days are number'd,
　Or his deeds since the days of his life began?

One, glad because of the light, saith, "Shall not
　The righteous Judge of all the earth do right,
For behold the sparrows on the house-tops fall not
　Save as seemeth to Him good in His sight?"
And this man's joy shall have no abiding,
Through lights departing and lives dividing,
He is soon as one in the darkness hiding,

One loving darkness rather than light.

A little season of love and laughter,
 Of light and life, and pleasure and pain,
And a horror of outer darkness after,
 And dust returneth to dust again.
Then the lesser life shall be as the greater,
And the lover of life shall join the hater,
And the one thing cometh sooner or later,
 And no one knoweth the loss or gain.

Love of my life! we had lights in season —
 Hard to part from, harder to keep —
We had strength to labour and souls to reason,
 And seed to scatter and fruits to reap.
Though time estranges and fate disperses,
We have HAD our loves and our loving mercies;
Though the gifts of the light in the end are curses,
 Yet bides the gift of the darkness — sleep!

See! girt with tempest and wing'd with thunder,
 And clad with lightning and shod with sleet,
The strong winds treading the swift waves sunder
 The flying rollers with frothy feet.
One gleam like a bloodshot sword-blade swims on
The sky-line, staining the green gulf crimson,
A death stroke fiercely dealt by a dim sun,
 That strikes through his stormy winding-sheet.

Oh! brave white horses! you gather and gallop,
 The storm sprite loosens the gusty reins;
Now the stoutest ship were the frailest shallop
 In your hollow backs, or your high arch'd manes.
I would ride as never a man has ridden
In your sleepy, swirling surges hidden,
To gulfs foreshadow'd through straits forbidden,
 Where no light wearies and no love wanes.

From the Wreck

"Turn out, boys!" — "What's up with our super. to-night?
 The man's mad — Two hours to daybreak I'd swear —
Stark mad — why, there isn't a glimmer of light."
"Take Bolingbroke, Alec, give Jack the young mare;
Look sharp. A large vessel lies jamm'd on the reef,
 And many on board still, and some wash'd on shore.
Ride straight with the news — they may send some relief
 From the township; and we — we can do little more.
You, Alec, you know the near cuts; you can cross
 'The Sugarloaf' ford with a scramble, I think;
Don't spare the blood filly, nor yet the black horse;
 Should the wind rise, God help them! the ship will soon sink.
Old Peter's away down the paddock, to drive
 The nags to the stockyard as fast as he can —
A life and death matter; so, lads, look alive."
Half-dress'd, in the dark, to the stockyard we ran.

There was bridling with hurry, and saddling with haste,
 Confusion and cursing for lack of a moon;
"Be quick with these buckles, we've no time to waste;"
 "Mind the mare, she can use her hind legs to some tune."
"Make sure of the crossing-place; strike the old track,
 They've fenced off the new one; look out for the holes
On the wombat hills." "Down with the slip rails; stand back."
 "And ride, boys, the pair of you, ride for your souls."

In the low branches heavily laden with dew,
 In the long grasses spoiling with deadwood that day,
Where the blackwood, the box, and the bastard oak grew,
 Between the tall gum-trees we gallop'd away —
We crash'd through a brush fence, we splash'd through a swamp —
 We steered for the north near "The Eaglehawk's Nest" —
We bore to the left, just beyond "The Red Camp",
 And round the black tea-tree belt wheel'd to the west —
We cross'd a low range sickly scented with musk
 From wattle-tree blossom — we skirted a marsh —

Then the dawn faintly dappled with orange the dusk,
 And peal'd overhead the jay's laughter note harsh,
And shot the first sunstreak behind us, and soon
 The dim dewy uplands were dreamy with light;
And full on our left flash'd "The Reedy Lagoon",
 And sharply "The Sugarloaf" rear'd on our right.
A smother'd curse broke through the bushman's brown beard,
 He turn'd in his saddle, his brick-colour'd cheek
Flush'd feebly with sundawn, said, "Just what I fear'd;
 Last fortnight's late rainfall has flooded the creek."

Black Bolingbroke snorted, and stood on the brink
 One instant, then deep in the dark sluggish swirl
Plunged headlong. I saw the horse suddenly sink,
 Till round the man's armpits the waves seemed to curl.
We follow'd, — one cold shock, and deeper we sank
 Than they did, and twice tried the landing in vain;
The third struggle won it; straight up the steep bank
 We stagger'd, then out on the skirts of the plain.

The stockrider, Alec, at starting had got
 The lead, and had kept it throughout; 'twas his boast
That through thickest of scrub he could steer like a shot,
 And the black horse was counted the best on the coast.
The mare had been awkward enough in the dark,
 She was eager and headstrong, and barely half broke;
She had had me too close to a big stringy-bark,
 And had made a near thing of a crooked sheoak;
But now on the open, lit up by the morn,
 She flung the white foam-flakes from nostril to neck,
And chased him — I hatless, with shirt sleeves all torn
 (For he may ride ragged who rides from a wreck) —
And faster and faster across the wide heath
 We rode till we raced. Then I gave her her head,
And she — stretching out with the bit in her teeth —
 She caught him, outpaced him, and passed him, and led.

We neared the new fence, we were wide of the track;
 I look'd right and left — she had never been tried
At a stiff leap; 'twas little he cared on the black.
 "You're more than a mile from the gateway," he cried.
I hung to her head, touched her flank with the spurs
 (In the red streak of rail not the ghost of a gap);

She shortened her long stroke, she pricked her sharp ears,
  She flung it behind her with hardly a rap —
I saw the post quiver where Bolingbroke struck,
  And guessed that the pace we had come the last mile
Had blown him a bit (he could jump like a buck).
We galloped more steadily then for a while.

The heath was soon pass'd, in the dim distance lay
  The mountain. The sun was just clearing the tips
Of the ranges to eastward. The mare — could she stay?
  She was bred very nearly as clean as Eclipse;
She led, and as oft as he came to her side,
  She took the bit free and untiring as yet;
Her neck was arched double, her nostrils were wide,
  And the tips of her tapering ears nearly met —
"You're lighter than I am," said Alec at last;
  "The horse is dead beat and the mare isn't blown.
She must be a good one — ride on and ride fast,
  You know your way now." So I rode on alone.

Still galloping forward we pass'd the two flocks
  At M'Intyre's hut and M'Allister's hill —
She was galloping strong at the Warrigal Rocks —
  On the Wallaby Range she was galloping still —
And over the wasteland and under the wood,
  By down and by dale, and by fell and by flat,
She gallop'd, and here in the stirrups I stood
  To ease her, and there in the saddle I sat
To steer her. We suddenly struck the red loam
  Of the track near the troughs — then she reeled on the rise —
From her crest to her croup covered over with foam,
  And blood-red her nostrils, and bloodshot her eyes,
A dip in the dell where the wattle fire bloomed —
  A bend round a bank that had shut out the view —
Large framed in the mild light the mountain had loomed,
  With a tall, purple peak bursting out from the blue.

I pull'd her together, I press'd her, and she
  Shot down the decline to the Company's yard,
And on by the paddocks, yet under my knee
  I could feel her heart thumping the saddle-flaps hard.
Yet a mile and another, and now we were near
  The goal, and the fields and the farms flitted past;

And 'twixt the two fences I turned with a cheer,
 For a green grass-fed mare 'twas a far thing and fast;
And labourers, roused by her galloping hoofs,
 Saw bare-headed rider and foam-sheeted steed;
And shone the white walls and the slate-coloured roofs
 Of the township. I steadied her then — I had need —
Where stood the old chapel (where stands the new church —
 Since chapels to churches have changed in that town).
A short, sidelong stagger, a long, forward lurch,
 A slight, choking sob, and the mare had gone down.
I slipp'd off the bridle, I slacken'd the girth,
 I ran on and left her and told them my news;
I saw her soon afterwards. What was she worth?
 How much for her hide? She had never worn shoes.

No Name

"A stone upon her heart and head,
 But no name written on that stone;
Sweet neighbours whisper low instead,
 This sinner was a loving one." — Mrs. Browning.

'Tis a nameless stone that stands at your head —
 The gusts in the gloomy gorges whirl
Brown leaves and red till they cover your bed —
 Now I trust that your sleep is a sound one, girl!

I said in my wrath, when his shadow cross'd
 From your garden gate to your cottage door,
"What does it matter for one soul lost?
 Millions of souls have been lost before."

Yet I warn'd you — ah! but my words came true —
 "Perhaps some day you will find him out."
He who was not worthy to loosen your shoe,
 Does his conscience therefore prick him? I doubt.

You laughed and were deaf to my warning voice —
 Blush'd and were blind to his cloven hoof —
You have had your chance, you have taken your choice
 How could I help you, standing aloof?

He has prosper'd well with the world — he says
 I am mad — if so, and if he be sane,
I, at least, give God thanksgiving and praise
 That there lies between us one difference plain.

   *   *   *   *   *

You in your beauty above me bent
 In the pause of a wild west country ball —
Spoke to me — touched me without intent —
 Made me your servant for once and all.

Light laughter rippled your rose-red lip,
  And you swept my cheek with a shining curl,
That stray'd from your shoulder's snowy tip —
  Now I pray that your sleep is a sound one, girl!

From a long way off to look at your charms
  Made my blood run redder in every vein,
And he — he has held you long in his arms,
  And has kiss'd you over and over again.

Is it well that he keeps well out of my way?
  If we met, he and I — we alone — we two —
Would I give him one moment's grace to pray?
  Not I, for the sake of the soul he slew.

A life like a shuttlecock may be toss'd
  With the hand of fate for a battledore;
But it matters much for your sweet soul lost,
  As much as a million souls and more.

And I know that if, here or there, alone,
  I found him, fairly and face to face,
Having slain his body, I would slay my own,
  That my soul to Satan his soul might chase.

He hardens his heart in the public way —
  Who am I? I am but a nameless churl;
But God will put all things straight some day —
  Till then may your sleep be a sound one, girl!

Wolf and Hound

"The hills like giants at a hunting lay
Chin upon hand, to see the game at bay." — Browning.

You'll take my tale with a little salt,
 But it needs none, nevertheless,
I was foil'd completely, fairly at fault,
 Dishearten'd, too, I confess.
At the splitters' tent I had seen the track
 Of horse-hoofs fresh on the sward,
And though Darby Lynch and Donovan Jack
 (Who could swear through a ten-inch board)
Solemnly swore he had not been there,
 I was just as sure that they lied,
For to Darby all that is foul was fair,
 And Jack for his life was tried.

We had run him for seven miles and more
 As hard as our nags could split;
At the start they were all too weary and sore,
 And his was quite fresh and fit.
Young Marsden's pony had had enough
 On the plain, where the chase was hot;
We breasted the swell of the Bittern's Bluff,
 And Mark couldn't raise a trot;
When the sea, like a splendid silver shield,
 To the south-west suddenly lay;
On the brow of the Beetle the chestnut reel'd,
 And I bid good-bye to M'Crea —
And I was alone when the mare fell lame,
 With a pointed flint in her shoe,
On the Stony Flats: I had lost the game,
 And what was a man to do?

I turned away with no fixed intent
 And headed for Hawthorndell;
I could neither eat in the splitters' tent,

Nor drink at the splitters' well;
I knew that they gloried in my mishap,
 And I cursed them between my teeth —
A blood-red sunset through Brayton's Gap
 Flung a lurid fire on the heath.

Could I reach the Dell? I had little reck,
 And with scarce a choice of my own
I threw the reins on Miladi's neck —
 I had freed her foot from the stone.
That season most of the swamps were dry,
 And after so hard a burst,
In the sultry noon of so hot a sky,
 She was keen to appease her thirst —
Or by instinct urged or impelled by fate —
 I care not to solve these things —
Certain it is that she took me straight
 To the Warrigal water springs.

I can shut my eyes and recall the ground
 As though it were yesterday —
With a shelf of the low, grey rocks girt round,
 The springs in their basin lay;
Woods to the east and wolds to the north
 In the sundown sullenly bloom'd;
Dead black on a curtain of crimson cloth
 Large peaks to the westward loomed.
I led Miladi through weed and sedge,
 She leisurely drank her fill;
There was something close to the water's edge,
 And my heart with one leap stood still,

For a horse's shoe and a rider's boot
 Had left clean prints on the clay;
Someone had watered his beast on foot.
 'Twas he — he had gone. Which way?
Then the mouth of the cavern faced me fair,
 As I turned and fronted the rocks;
So, at last, I had pressed the wolf to his lair,
 I had run to his earth the fox.

I thought so. Perhaps he was resting. Perhaps
 He was waiting, watching for me.

I examined all my revolver caps,
  I hitched my mare to a tree —
I had sworn to have him, alive or dead,
  And to give him a chance was loth.
He knew his life had been forfeited —
  He had even heard of my oath.
In my stocking soles to the shelf I crept,
  I crawl'd safe into the cave —
All silent — if he was there he slept
  Not there. All dark as the grave.

Through the crack I could hear the leaden hiss!
  See the livid face through the flame!
How strange it seems that a man should miss
  When his life depends on his aim!
There couldn't have been a better light
  For him, nor a worse for me.
We were coop'd up, caged like beasts for a fight,
  And dumb as dumb beasts were we.

Flash! flash! bang! bang! and we blazed away,
  And the grey roof reddened and rang;
Flash! flash! and I felt his bullet flay
  The tip of my ear. Flash! bang!
Bang! flash! and my pistol arm fell broke;
  I struck with my left hand then —
Struck at a corpse through a cloud of smoke —
  I had shot him dead in his den!

De Te

A burning glass of burnished brass,
  The calm sea caught the noontide rays,
And sunny slopes of golden grass
  And wastes of weed-flower seem to blaze.
Beyond the shining silver-greys,
  Beyond the shades of denser bloom,
The sky-line girt with glowing haze
  The farthest, faintest forest gloom,
  And the everlasting hills that loom.

We heard the hound beneath the mound,
  We scared the swamp hawk hovering nigh —
We had not sought for that we found —
  He lay as dead men only lie,
With wan cheek whitening in the sky,
  Through the wild heath flowers, white and red,
The dumb brute that had seen him die,
  Close crouching, howl'd beside the head,
  Brute burial service o'er the dead.

The brow was rife with seams of strife —
  A lawless death made doubly plain
The ravage of a reckless life;
  The havoc of a hurricane
Of passions through that breadth of brain,
  Like headlong horses that had run
Riot, regardless of the rein —
  "Madman, he might have lived and done
  Better than most men," whispered one.

The beams and blots that Heaven allots
  To every life with life begin.
Fool! would you change the leopard's spots,
  Or blanch the Ethiopian's skin?
What more could he have hoped to win,
  What better things have thought to gain,

So shapen — so conceived in sin?
 No life is wholly void and vain,
 Just and unjust share sun and rain.

Were new life sent, and life misspent,
 Wiped out (if such to God seemed good),
 Would he (being as he was) repent,
 Or could he, even if he would,
Who heeded not things understood
 (Though dimly) even in savage lands
By some who worship stone or wood,
 Or bird or beast, or who stretch hands
 Sunward on shining Eastern sands?

And crime has cause. Nay, never pause
 Idly to feel a pulseless wrist;
Brace up the massive, square-shaped jaws,
 Unclench the stubborn, stiff'ning fist,
And close those eyes through film and mist
 That kept the old defiant glare;
And answer, wise Psychologist,
 Whose science claims some little share
 Of truth, what better things lay there?

Aye! thought and mind were there, — some kind
 Of faculty that men mistake
For talent when their wits are blind, —
 An aptitude to mar and break
What others diligently make.
 This was the worst and best of him —
Wise with the cunning of the snake,
 Brave with the she wolf's courage grim,
 Dying hard and dumb, torn limb from limb.

And you, Brown, you're a doctor; cure
 You can't, but you can kill, and he —
"WITNESS HIS MARK" — he signed last year,
 And now he signs John Smith, J.P.
We'll hold our inquest NOW, we three;
 I'll be your coroner for once;
I think old Oswald ought to be
 Our foreman — Jones is such a dunce, —
 There's more brain in the bloodhound's sconce.

No man may shirk the allotted work,
 The deed to do, the death to die;
At least I think so, — neither Turk,
 Nor Jew, nor infidel am I, —
And yet I wonder when I try
 To solve one question, may or must,
And shall I solve it by-and-by,
 Beyond the dark, beneath the dust?
 I trust so, and I only trust.

Aye, what they will, such trifles kill.
 Comrade, for one good deed of yours,
Your history shall not help to fill
 The mouths of many brainless boors.
It may be death absolves or cures
 The sin of life. 'Twere hazardous
To assert so. If the sin endures,
 Say only, "God, who has judged him thus,
 Be merciful to him and us."

How we Beat the Favourite

A Lay of the Loamshire Hunt Cup

"Aye, squire," said Stevens, "they back him at evens;
  The race is all over, bar shouting, they say;
The Clown ought to beat her; Dick Neville is sweeter
  Than ever — he swears he can win all the way.

"A gentleman rider — well, I'm an outsider,
  But if he's a gent who the mischief's a jock?
You swells mostly blunder, Dick rides for the plunder,
  He rides, too, like thunder — he sits like a rock.

"He calls 'hunted fairly' a horse that has barely
  Been stripp'd for a trot within sight of the hounds,
A horse that at Warwick beat Birdlime and Yorick,
  And gave Abdelkader at Aintree nine pounds.

"They say we have no test to warrant a protest;
  Dick rides for a lord and stands in with a steward;
The light of their faces they show him — his case is
  Prejudged and his verdict already secured.

"But none can outlast her, and few travel faster,
  She strides in her work clean away from The Drag;
You hold her and sit her, she couldn't be fitter,
  Whenever you hit her she'll spring like a stag.

"And p'rhaps the green jacket, at odds though they back it,
  May fall, or there's no knowing what may turn up;
The mare is quite ready, sit still and ride steady,
  Keep cool; and I think you may just win the Cup."

Dark-brown with tan muzzle, just stripped for the tussle,
  Stood Iseult, arching her neck to the curb,
A lean head and fiery, strong quarters and wiry,
  A loin rather light, but a shoulder superb.

Some parting injunction, bestowed with great unction,
I tried to recall, but forgot like a dunce,
When Reginald Murray, full tilt on White Surrey,
Came down in a hurry to start us at once.

"Keep back in the yellow! Come up on Othello!
Hold hard on the chestnut! Turn round on The Drag!
Keep back there on Spartan! Back you, sir, in tartan!
So, steady there, easy!" and down went the flag.

We started, and Kerr made strong running on Mermaid,
Through furrows that led to the first stake-and-bound,
The crack, half extended, look'd bloodlike and splendid,
Held wide on the right where the headland was sound.

I pulled hard to baffle her rush with the snaffle,
Before her two-thirds of the field got away,
All through the wet pasture where floods of the last year
Still loitered, they clotted my crimson with clay.

The fourth fence, a wattle, floor'd Monk and Bluebottle;
The Drag came to grief at the blackthorn and ditch,
The rails toppled over Redoubt and Red Rover,
The lane stopped Lycurgus and Leicestershire Witch.

She passed like an arrow Kildare and Cock Sparrow,
And Mantrap and Mermaid refused the stone wall;
And Giles on The Greyling came down at the paling,
And I was left sailing in front of them all.

I took them a burster, nor eased her nor nursed her
Until the Black Bullfinch led into the plough,
And through the strong bramble we bored with a scramble —
My cap was knock'd off by the hazel-tree bough.

Where furrows looked lighter I drew the rein tighter —
Her dark chest all dappled with flakes of white foam,
Her flanks mud-bespattered, a weak rail she shattered —
We landed on turf with our heads turn'd for home.

Then crash'd a low binder, and then close behind her
The sward to the strokes of the favourite shook;
His rush roused her mettle, yet ever so little

She shortened her stride as we raced at the brook.

She rose when I hit her. I saw the stream glitter,
 A wide scarlet nostril flashed close to my knee,
Between sky and water The Clown came and caught her,
 The space that he cleared was a caution to see.

And forcing the running, discarding all cunning,
 A length to the front went the rider in green;
A long strip of stubble, and then the big double,
 Two stiff flights of rails with a quickset between.

She raced at the rasper, I felt my knees grasp her,
 I found my hands give to her strain on the bit;
She rose when The Clown did — our silks as we bounded
 Brush'd lightly, our stirrups clash'd loud as we lit.

A rise steeply sloping, a fence with stone coping —
 The last — we diverged round the base of the hill;
His path was the nearer, his leap was the clearer,
 I flogg'd up the straight, and he led sitting still.

She came to his quarter, and on still I brought her,
 And up to his girth, to his breastplate she drew;
A short prayer from Neville just reach'd me, "The devil!"
 He mutter'd — lock'd level the hurdles we flew.

A hum of hoarse cheering, a dense crowd careering,
 All sights seen obscurely, all shouts vaguely heard;
"The green wins!" "The crimson!" The multitude swims on,
 And figures are blended and features are blurr'd.

"The horse is her master!" "The green forges past her!"
 "The Clown will outlast her!" "The Clown wins!" "The Clown!"
The white railing races with all the white faces,
 The chestnut outpaces, outstretches the brown.

On still past the gateway she strains in the straightway,
 Still struggles, "The Clown by a short neck at most,"
He swerves, the green scourges, the stand rocks and surges,
 And flashes, and verges, and flits the white post.

Aye! so ends the tussle, — I knew the tan muzzle

Was first, though the ring-men were yelling "Dead heat!"
A nose I could swear by, but Clarke said, "The mare by
A short head." And that's how the favourite was beat.

Fragmentary Scenes from the Road to Avernus

An Unpublished Dramatic Lyric

Scene I
"Discontent"

LAURENCE RABY.

Laurence:
I said to young Allan M'Ilveray,
 Beside the swift swirls of the North,
When, in lilac shot through with a silver ray,
 We haul'd the strong salmon fish forth —
Said only, "He gave us some trouble
 To land him, and what does he weigh?
Our friend has caught one that weighs double,
 The game for the candle won't pay
  Us to-day,
We may tie up our rods and away."

I said to old Norman M'Gregor,
 Three leagues to the west of Glen Dhu —
I had drawn, with a touch of the trigger,
 The best BEAD that ever I drew —
Said merely, "For birds in the stubble
 I once had an eye — I could swear
He's down — but he's not worth the trouble
 Of seeking. You once shot a bear
  In his lair —
'Tis only a buck that lies there."

I said to Lord Charles only last year,
 The time that we topp'd the oak rail
Between Wharton's plough and Whynne's pasture,
 And clear'd the big brook in Blakesvale —

We only — at Warburton's double
He fell, then I finish'd the run
And kill'd clean — said, "So bursts a bubble
That shone half an hour in the sun —
        What is won?
Your sire clear'd and captured a gun."

I said to myself, in true sorrow,
 I said yestere'en, "A fair prize
Is won, and it may be to-morrow
 'Twill not seem so fair in thine eyes —
Real life is a race through sore trouble,
 That gains not an inch on the goal,
And bliss an intangible bubble
 That cheats an unsatisfied soul,
        And the whole
Of the rest an illegible scroll."

Scene VII
"Two Exhortations"

A Shooting-box in the West of Ireland. A Bedchamber.
LAURENCE RABY and MELCHIOR. Night.

Melchior:
Surely in the great beginning God made all things good, and still
That soul-sickness men call sinning entered not without His will.
Nay, our wisest have asserted that, as shade enhances light,
Evil is but good perverted, wrong is but the foil of right.
Banish sickness, then you banish joy for health to all that live;
Slay all sin, all good must vanish, good being but comparative.
Sophistry, you say — yet listen: look you skyward, there 'tis known
Worlds on worlds in myriads glisten — larger, lovelier than our own —
This has been, and this still shall be, here as there, in sun or star;
These things are to be and will be, those things were to be and are.
Man in man's imperfect nature is by imperfection taught:
Add one cubit to your stature if you can by taking thought.

Laurence:
Thus you would not teach that peasant, though he calls you "father".

Melchior: True,
I should magnify this present, mystify that future, too —
We adapt our conversation always to our hearer's light.

Laurence:
I am not of your persuasion.

Melchior: Yet the difference is but slight.

Laurence:
I, EVEN I, say, "He who barters worldly weal for heavenly worth
He does well" — your saints and martyrs were examples here on earth.

Melchior:
Aye, in earlier Christian ages, while the heathen empire stood,
When the war 'twixt saints and sages cried aloud for saintly blood,
Christ was then their model truly. Now, if all were meek and pure,
Save the ungodly and the unruly, would the Christian Church endure?
Shall the toiler or the fighter dream by day and watch by night,
Turn the left cheek to the smiter, smitten rudely on the right?
Strong men must encounter bad men — so-called saints of latter days
Have been mostly pious madmen, lusting after righteous praise —
Or the thralls of superstition, doubtless worthy some reward,
Since they came by their condition hardly of their free accord.
'Tis but madness, sad and solemn, that these fakir-Christians feel —
Saint Stylites on his column gratified a morbid zeal.

Laurence:
By your showing, good is really on a par (of worth) with ill.

Melchior:
Nay, I said not so; I merely tell you both some ends fulfil —
Priestly vows were my vocation, fast and vigil wait for me.
You must work and face temptation. Never should the strong man flee,
Though God wills the inclination with the soul at war to be.
    (Pauses.)

In the strife 'twixt flesh and spirit, while you can the spirit aid.
Should you fall not less your merit, be not for a fall afraid.
Whatsoe'er most right, most fit is you shall do. When all is done
Chaunt the noble Nunc Dimittis — Benedicimur, my son.
    [Exit MELCHIOR.]

Laurence (alone):
Why do I provoke these wrangles? Melchior talks (as well he may)
With the tongues of men and angels.
(Takes up a pamphlet.) What has this man got to say?
(Reads.) Sic sacerdos fatur (ejus nomen quondam erat Burgo.)
Mala mens est, caro pejus, anima infirma, ergo
I nunc, ora, sine mora — orat etiam Sancta Virgo.
(Thinks.)
(Speaks.) So it seems they mean to make her wed the usurer, Nathan
    Lee.
Poor Estelle! her friends forsake her; what has this to do with me?
Glad I am, at least, that Helen still refuses to discard
Her, through tales false gossips tell
  in spite or heedlessness. — 'Tis hard! —
Lee, the Levite! — some few years back Herbert horsewhipp'd him
  — the cur
Show'd his teeth and laid his ears back. Now his wealth has
    purchased her.
Must his baseness mar her brightness? Shall the callous, cunning
    churl
Revel in the rosy whiteness of that golden-headed girl?
(Thinks and smokes.)
(Reads.) Cito certe venit vitae finis (sic sacerdos fatur),
Nunc audite omnes, ite, vobis fabula narratur
Nunc orate et laudate, laudat etiam Alma Mater.
(Muses.) Such has been, and such shall still be,
  here as there, in sun or star;
These things are to be and will be, those things were to be and are.
If I thought that speech worth heeding I should — Nay, it seems to
    me
More like Satan's special pleading than like Gloria Domine.
(Lies down on his couch.)
(Reads.) Et tuquoque frater meus facta mala quod fecisti
Denique confundit Deus omnes res quas tetegisti.
Nunc si unquam, nunc aut nunquam, sanguine adjuro Christi.

Scene IX
"In the Garden"

Aylmer's Garden, near the Lake. LAURENCE RABY and ESTELLE.

He:
Come to the bank where the boat is moor'd to the willow-tree low;
Bertha, the baby, won't notice, Brian, the blockhead, won't know.

She:
Bertha is not such a baby, sir, as you seem to suppose;
Brian, a blockhead he may be, more than you think for he knows.

He:
This much, at least, of your brother, from the beginning he knew
Somewhat concerning that other made such a fool of by you.

She:
Firmer those bonds were and faster, Frank was my spaniel, my slave.
You! you would fain be my master; mark you! the difference is
    grave.

He:
Call me your spaniel, your starling, take me and treat me as these,
I would be anything, darling! aye, whatsoever you please.
Brian and Basil are "punting", leave them their dice and their wine,
Bertha is butterfly hunting, surely one hour shall be mine.
See, I have done with all duty; see, I can dare all disgrace,
Only to look at your beauty, feasting my eyes on your face.

She:
Look at me, aye, till your eyes ache! How, let me ask, will it end?
Neither for your sake, nor my sake, but for the sake of my friend?

He:
Is she your friend then? I own it, this is all wrong, and the rest,
Frustra sed anima monet, caro quod fortius est.

She:
Not quite so close, Laurence Raby, not with your arm round my
    waist;

Something to look at I may be, nothing to touch or to taste.

He:
Wilful as ever and wayward; why did you tempt me, Estelle?

She:
You misinterpret each stray word, you for each inch take an ell.
Lightly all laws and ties trammel me, I am warn'd for all that.

He (aside):
Perhaps she will swallow her camel when she has strained at her
　　gnat.

She:
Therefore take thought and consider, weigh well, as I do, the whole,
You for mere beauty a bidder, say, would you barter a soul?

He:
Girl! THAT MAY happen, but THIS IS; after this welcome the worst;
Blest for one hour by your kisses, let me be evermore curs'd.
Talk not of ties to me reckless, here every tie I discard —
Make me your girdle, your necklace —

She:　　　　　　　　Laurence, you kiss me too hard.

He:
Aye, 'tis the road to Avernus, n'est ce pas vrai donc, ma belle?
There let them bind us or burn us, mais le jeu vaut la chandelle.
Am I your lord or your vassal? Are you my sun or my torch?
You, when I look at you, dazzle, yet when I touch you, you scorch.

She:
Yonder are Brian and Basil watching us fools from the porch.

Scene X
"After the Quarrel"

Laurence Raby's Chamber. LAURENCE enters, a little the worse for
　　liquor.

Laurence:
He never gave me a chance to speak,
 And he call'd her — worse than a dog —
The girl stood up with a crimson cheek,
 And I fell'd him there like a log.

I can feel the blow on my knuckles yet —
 He feels it more on his brow.
In a thousand years we shall all forget
 The things that trouble us now.

Scene XI
"Ten Paces Off"

An open country.   LAURENCE RABY and FORREST, BRIAN AYLMER and PRESCOT.

Forrest:
I've won the two tosses from Prescot;
 Now hear me, and hearken and heed,
And pull that vile flower from your waistcoat,
 And throw down that beast of a weed;
I'm going to give you the signal
 I gave Harry Hunt at Boulogne,
The morning he met Major Bignell,
 And shot him as dead as a stone;
For he must look round on his right hand
 To watch the white flutter — that stops
His aim, for it takes off his sight, and
 I COUGH WHILE THE HANDKERCHIEF DROPS.
And you keep both eyes on his figure,
 Old fellow, and don't take them off.
You've got the sawhandled hair trigger —
 You sight him and shoot when I cough.

Laurence (aside):
Though God will never forgive me,
 Though men make light of my name,

Though my sin and my shame outlive me,
 I shall not outlast my shame.
The coward, does he mean to miss me?
 His right hand shakes like a leaf;
Shall I live for my friends to hiss me,
 Of fools and of knaves the chief?
Shall I live for my foes to twit me?
 He has master'd his nerve again —
He is firm, he will surely hit me —
 Will he reach the heart or the brain?
One long look eastward and northward —
 One prayer — "Our Father which art" —
And the cough chimes in with the fourth word,
 And I shoot skyward — the heart.

Last Scene
"Exeunt"

HELEN RABY.

Where the grave-deeps rot, where the grave-dews rust,
 They dug, crying, "Earth to earth" —
Crying, "Ashes to ashes and dust to dust" —
 And what are my poor prayers worth?
Upon whom shall I call, or in whom shall I trust,
 Though death were indeed new birth.

And they bid me be glad for my baby's sake
 That she suffered sinless and young —
Would they have me be glad when my breasts still ache
 Where that small, soft, sweet mouth clung?
I am glad that the heart will so surely break
 That has been so bitterly wrung.

He was false, they tell me, and what if he were?
 I can only shudder and pray,
Pouring out my soul in a passionate prayer
 For the soul that he cast away;

Was there nothing that once was created fair
 In the potter's perishing clay?

Is it well for the sinner that souls endure?
 For the sinless soul is it well?
Does the pure child lisp to the angels pure?
 And where does the strong man dwell,
If the sad assurance of priests be sure,
 Or the tale that our preachers tell?

The unclean has follow'd the undefiled,
 And the ill MAY regain the good,
And the man MAY be even as the little child!
 We are children lost in the wood —
Lord! lead us out of this tangled wild,
Where the wise and the prudent have been beguil'd,
 And only the babes have stood.

Doubtful Dreams

Aye, snows are rife in December,
 And sheaves are in August yet,
And you would have me remember,
 And I would rather forget;
In the bloom of the May-day weather,
 In the blight of October chill,
We were dreamers of old together, —
 As of old, are you dreaming still?

For nothing on earth is sadder
 Than the dream that cheated the grasp,
The flower that turned to the adder,
 The fruit that changed to the asp;
When the day-spring in darkness closes,
 As the sunset fades from the hills,
With the fragrance of perish'd roses,
 With the music of parch'd-up rills.

When the sands on the sea-shore nourish
 Red clover and yellow corn;
When figs on the thistle flourish,
 And grapes grow thick on the thorn;
When the dead branch, blighted and blasted,
 Puts forth green leaves in the spring,
Then the dream that life has outlasted
 Dead comfort to life may bring.

I have changed the soil and the season,
 But whether skies freeze or flame,
The soil they flame on or freeze on
 Is changed in little save name;
The loadstone points to the nor'ward,
 The river runs to the sea;
And you would have me look forward,
 And backward I fain would flee.

I remember the bright spring garlands,
  The gold that spangled the green,
And the purple on fairy far lands,
  And the white and the red bloom, seen
From the spot where we last lay dreaming
  Together — yourself and I —
The soft grass beneath us gleaming,
  Above us the great grave sky.

And we spoke thus: "Though we have trodden
  Rough paths in our boyish years;
And some with our sweat are sodden,
  And some are salt with our tears;
Though we stumble still, walking blindly,
  Our paths shall be made all straight;
We are weak, but the heavens are kindly,
  The skies are compassionate."

Is the clime of the old land younger,
  Where the young dreams longer are nursed?
With the old insatiable hunger,
  With the old unquenchable thirst,
Are you longing, as in the old years
  We have longed so often in vain;
Fellow-toilers still, fellow-soldiers,
  Though the seas have sundered us twain?

But the young dreams surely have faded!
  Young dreams! — old dreams of young days —
Shall the new dream vex us as they did?
  Or as things worth censure or praise?
Real toil is ours, real trouble,
  Dim dreams of pleasure and pride;
Let the dreams disperse like a bubble,
  So the toil like a dream subside.

Vain toil! men better and braver
  Rose early and rested late,
Whose burdens than ours were graver,
  And sterner than ours their hate.
What fair reward had Achilles?
  What rest could Alcides win?
Vain toil! "Consider the lilies,

They toil not neither do spin."

Nor for mortal toiling nor spinning
  Will the matters of mortals mend;
As it was so in the beginning,
  It shall be so in the end.
The web that the weavers weave ill
  Shall not be woven aright
Till the good is brought forth from evil,
  As day is brought forth from night.

Vain dreams! for our fathers cherish'd
  High hopes in the days that were;
And these men wonder'd and perish'd,
  Nor better than these we fare;
And our due at last is their due,
  They fought against odds and fell;
"En avant, les enfants perdus!"
  We fight against odds as well.

The skies! Will the great skies care for
  Our footsteps, straighten our path,
Or strengthen our weakness? Wherefore?
  We have rather incurr'd their wrath;
When against the Captain of Hazor
  The stars in their courses fought,
Did the skies shed merciful rays, or
  With love was the sunshine fraught?

Can they favour man? Can they wrong man?
  The unapproachable skies?
Though these gave strength to the strong man,
  And wisdom gave to the wise;
When strength is turn'd to derision,
  And wisdom brought to dismay,
Shall we wake from a troubled vision,
  Or rest from a toilsome day?

Nay! I cannot tell. Peradventure
  Our very toil is a dream,
And the works that we praise or censure,
  It may be, they only seem.
If so, I would fain awaken,

Or sleep more soundly than so,
 Or by dreamless sleep overtaken,
The dream I would fain forego.

For the great things of earth are small things,
 The longest life is a span,
And there is an end to all things,
 A season to every man,
Whose glory is dust and ashes,
 Whose spirit is but a spark,
That out from the darkness flashes,
 And flickers out in the dark.

We remember the pangs that wrung us
 When some went down to the pit,
Who faded as leaves among us,
 Who flitted as shadows flit;
What visions under the stone lie?
 What dreams in the shroud sleep dwell?
For we saw the earth pit only,
 And we heard only the knell.

We know not whether they slumber
 Who waken on earth no more,
As the stars of the heights in number,
 As sands on the deep sea-shore.
Shall stiffness bind them, and starkness
 Enthral them, by field and flood,
Till "the sun shall be turn'd to darkness,
 And the moon shall be turn'd to blood."

We know not! — worse may enthral men —
 "The wages of sin are death";
And so death passed upon all men,
 For sin was born with man's breath.
Then the labourer spent with sinning,
 His hire with his life shall spend;
For it was so in the beginning,
 And shall be so in the end.

There is life in the blacken'd ember
 While a spark is smouldering yet;
In a dream e'en now I remember

That dream I had lief forget —
I had lief forget, I had e'en lief
That dream with THIS doubt should die —
"IF WE DID THESE THINGS IN THE GREEN LEAF,
WHAT SHALL BE DONE IN THE DRY?"

The Rhyme of Joyous Garde

Through the lattice rushes the south wind, dense
With fumes of the flowery frankincense
   From hawthorn blossoming thickly;
And gold is shower'd on grass unshorn,
And poppy-fire on shuddering corn,
With May-dew flooded and flush'd with morn,
   And scented with sweetness sickly.

The bloom and brilliance of summer days,
The buds that brighten, the fields that blaze,
   The fruits that ripen and redden,
And all the gifts of a God-sent light
Are sadder things in my shameful sight
Than the blackest gloom of the bitterest night,
   When the senses darken and deaden.

For the days recall what the nights efface,
Scenes of glory and seasons of grace,
   For which there is no returning —
Else the days were even as the nights to me,
Now the axe is laid to the root of the tree,
And to-morrow the barren trunk may be
   Cut down — cast forth for the burning.

Would God I had died the death that day
When the bishop blessed us before the fray
   At the shrine of the Saviour's Mother;
We buckled the spur, we braced the belt,
Arthur and I — together we knelt,
And the grasp of his kingly hand I felt
   As the grasp of an only brother.

The body and the blood of Christ we shared,
Knees bended and heads bow'd down and bared,
   We listened throughout the praying.
Eftsoon the shock of the foe we bore,

Shoulder to shoulder on Severn's shore,
Till our hilts were glued to our hands with gore,
   And our sinews slacken'd with slaying.

Was I far from Thy Kingdom, gracious Lord,
With a shattered casque and a shiver'd sword,
   On the threshold of Mary's chapel?
Pardie! I had well-nigh won that crown
Which endureth more than a knight's renown,
When the pagan giant had got me down,
   Sore spent in the deadly grapple.

May his craven spirit find little grace,
He was seal'd to Satan in any case,
   Yet the loser had been the winner;
Had I waxed fainter or he less faint,
Then my soul was free from this loathsome taint,
I had died as a Christian knight — no saint
   Perchance, yet a pardon'd sinner.

But I strove full grimly beneath his weight,
I clung to his poignard desperate,
   I baffled the thrust that followed,
And writhing uppermost rose, to deal,
With bare three inches of broken steel,
One stroke — Ha! the headpiece crash'd piecemeal,
   And the knave in his black blood wallow'd.

So I lived for worse — in fulness of time,
When peace for a season sway'd the clime,
   And spears for a space were idle,
Trusted and chosen of all the court,
A favoured herald of fair report,
I travell'd eastward, and duly brought
   A bride to a queenly bridal.

Pardie! 'twas a morning even as this
(The skies were warmer if aught, I wis,
   Albeit the fields were duller;
Or it may be that the envious spring,
Abash'd at the sight of a fairer thing,
Wax'd somewhat sadder of colouring
   Because of her faultless colour).

With her through the Lyonesse I rode,
Till the woods with the noontide fervour glow'd,
   And there for a space we halted,
Where the intertwining branches made
Cool carpets of olive-tinted shade,
And the floors with fretwork of flame inlaid
   From leafy lattices vaulted.

And scarf and mantle for her I spread,
And strewed them over the grassiest bed,
   And under the greenest awning,
And loosen'd latch and buckle, and freed
From selle and housing the red roan steed,
And the jennet of swift Iberian breed,
   That had carried us since the dawning.

The brown thrush sang through the briar and bower,
All flush'd or frosted with forest flower
   In the warm sun's wanton glances;
And I grew deaf to the song bird — blind
To blossom that sweeten'd the sweet spring wind —
I saw her only — a girl reclined
   In her girlhood's indolent trances.

And the song and the scent and sense wax'd weak,
The wild rose withered beside the cheek
   She poised on her fingers slender;
The soft spun gold of her glittering hair
Ran rippling into a wondrous snare,
That flooded the round arm bright and bare,
   And the shoulder's silvery splendour.

The deep dusk fires in those dreamy eyes,
Like seas clear-coloured in summer skies,
   Were guiltless of future treason;
And I stood watching her, still and mute,
Yet the evil seed in my soul found root,
And the sad plant throve, and the sinful fruit
   Grew ripe in the shameful season.

Let the sin be mine as the shame was hers,
In desolate days of departed years
   She had leisure for shame and sorrow —

There was light repentance and brief remorse,
When I rode against Saxon foes or Norse,
With clang of harness and clatter of horse,
   And little heed for the morrow.

And now she is dead, men tell me, and I,
In this living death must I linger and lie
   Till my cup to the dregs is drunken?
I looked through the lattice worn and grim,
With eyelids darken'd and eyesight dim,
And weary body and wasted limb,
   And sinew slacken'd and shrunken.

She is dead! Gone down to the burial-place,
Where the grave-dews cleave to her faultless face;
   Where the grave-sods crumble around her;
And that bright burden of burnish'd gold,
That once on those waxen shoulders roll'd,
Will it spoil with the damps of the deadly mould?
   Was it shorn when the church vows bound her?

Now I know full well that the fair spear shaft
Shall never gladden my hand, nor the haft
   Of the good sword grow to my fingers;
Now the maddest fray, the merriest din,
Would fail to quicken this life-stream thin,
Yet the sleepy poison of that sweet sin
   In the sluggish current still lingers.

Would God I had slept with the slain men, long
Or ever the heart conceived a wrong
   That the innermost soul abhorred —
Or ever these lying lips were strained
To her lids, pearl-tinted and purple-vein'd,
Or ever those traitorous kisses stained
   The snows of her spotless forehead.

Let me gather a little strength to think,
As one who reels on the outermost brink,
   To the innermost gulf descending.
In that truce the longest and last of all,
In the summer nights of that festival —
Soft vesture of samite and silken pall —

The beginning came of the ending.

And one trod softly with sandal'd feet —
Ah! why are the stolen waters sweet? —
   And one crept stealthily after;
I would I had taken him there and wrung
His knavish neck when the dark door swung,
Or torn by the roots his treacherous tongue,
   And stifled his hateful laughter.

So the smouldering scandal blazed — but he,
My king, to the last put trust in me —
   Aye, well was his trust requited!
Now priests may patter, and bells may toll,
He will need no masses to aid his soul;
When the angels open the judgment scroll,
   His wrong will be tenfold righted.

Then dawn'd the day when the mail was donn'd,
And the steed for the strife caparison'd,
   But not 'gainst the Norse invader.
Then was bloodshed — not by untoward chance,
As the blood that is drawn by the jouster's lance,
The fray in the castle of Melegrance,
   The fight in the lists with Mador.

Then the guilt made manifest, then the siege,
When the true men rallying round the liege
   Beleaguer'd his base betrayer;
Then the fruitless parleys, the pleadings vain,
And the hard-fought battles with brave Gawaine,
Twice worsted, and once so nearly slain,
   I may well be counted his slayer.

Then the crime of Modred — a little sin
At the side of mine, though the knave was kin
   To the king by the knave's hand stricken.
And the once-loved knight, was he there to save
That knightly king who that knighthood gave?
Ah, Christ! will he greet me as knight or knave
   In the day when the dust shall quicken.

Had he lightly loved, had he trusted less,

I had sinn'd perchance with the sinfulness
   That through prayer and penance is pardoned.
Oh, love most loyal! Oh, faith most sure!
In the purity of a soul so pure
I found my safeguard — I sinn'd secure,
   Till my heart to the sin grew harden'd.

We were glad together in gladsome meads,
When they shook to the strokes of our snorting steeds;
   We were joyful in joyous lustre
When it flush'd the coppice or fill'd the glade,
Where the horn of the Dane or the Saxon bray'd,
And we saw the heathen banner display'd,
   And the heathen lances cluster.

Then a steel-shod rush and a steel-clad ring,
And a crash of the spear staves splintering,
   And the billowy battle blended.
Riot of chargers, revel of blows,
And fierce, flush'd faces of fighting foes,
From croup to bridle, that reel'd and rose,
   In a sparkle of sword-play splendid.

And the long, lithe sword in the hand became
As a leaping light, as a falling flame,
   As a fire through the flax that hasted;
Slender, and shining, and beautiful,
How it shore through shivering casque and skull,
And never a stroke was void and null,
   And never a thrust was wasted.

I have done for ever with all these things —
Deeds that were joyous to knights and kings,
   In days that with songs were cherish'd.
The songs are ended, the deeds are done,
There shall none of them gladden me now, not one;
There is nothing good for me under the sun,
   But to perish as these things perish'd.

Shall it profit me aught that the bishop seeks
My presence daily, and duly speaks
   Soft words of comfort and kindness?
Shall it aught avail me? "Certes," he said,

"Though thy soul is darken'd, be not afraid —
God hateth nothing that He hath made —
   His light shall disperse thy blindness."

I am not afraid for myself, although
I know I have had that light, and I know
   The greater my condemnation.
When I well-nigh swoon'd in the deep-drawn bliss
Of that first long, sweet, slow, stolen kiss,
I would gladly have given, for less than this,
   Myself, with my soul's salvation.

I would languish thus in some loathsome den,
As a thing of naught in the eyes of men,
   In the mouths of men as a by-word,
Through years of pain, and when God saw fit,
Singing his praises my soul should flit
To the darkest depth of the nethermost pit,
   If HERS could be wafted skyward.

Lord Christ! have patience a little while,
I have sinn'd because I am utterly vile,
   Having light, loving darkness rather.
And I pray Thee deal with me as Thou wilt,
Yet the blood of Thy foes I have freely spilt,
And, moreover, mine is the greater guilt
   In the sight of Thee and Thy Father.

That saint, Thy servant, was counted dear
Whose sword in the garden grazed the ear
   Of Thine enemy, Lord Redeemer!
Not thus on the shattering visor jarr'd
In this hand the iron of the hilt cross-barr'd,
When the blade was swallow'd up to the guard
   Through the teeth of the strong blasphemer.

If ever I smote as a man should smite,
If I struck one stroke that seem'd good in Thy sight,
   By Thy loving mercy prevailing,
Lord! let her stand in the light of Thy face,
Cloth'd with Thy love and crown'd with Thy grace,
When I gnash my teeth in the terrible place
   That is fill'd with weeping and wailing.

Shall I comfort my soul on account of this?
In the world to come, whatsoever it is,
   There is no more earthly ill-doing —
For the dusty darkness shall slay desire,
And the chaff may burn with unquenchable fire,
But for green wild growth of thistle and briar
   At least there is no renewing.

And this grievous burden of life shall change
In the dim hereafter, dreamy and strange,
   And sorrows and joys diurnal.
And partial blessings and perishing ills
Shall fade in the praise, or the pang that fills
The glory of God's eternal hills,
   Or the gloom of His gulf eternal.

Yet if all things change to the glory of One
Who for all ill-doers gave His Own sweet Son,
   To His goodness so shall He change ill,
When the world as a wither'd leaf shall be,
And the sky like a shrivell'd scroll shall flee,
And souls shall be summon'd from land and sea,
   At the blast of His bright archangel.

Thora's Song
("Ashtaroth")

We severed in autumn early,
 Ere the earth was torn by the plough;
The wheat and the oats and the barley
 Are ripe for the harvest now.
We sunder'd one misty morning,
 Ere the hills were dimm'd by the rain,
Through the flowers those hills adorning —
 Thou comest not back again.

My heart is heavy and weary
 With the weight of a weary soul;
The mid-day glare grows dreary,
 And dreary the midnight scroll.
The corn-stalks sigh for the sickle,
 'Neath the load of the golden grain;
I sigh for a mate more fickle —
 Thou comest not back again.

The warm sun riseth and setteth,
 The night bringeth moist'ning dew,
But the soul that longeth forgetteth
 The warmth and the moisture, too;
In the hot sun rising and setting
 There is naught save feverish pain;
There are tears in the night-dews wetting —
 Thou comest not back again.

Thy voice in mine ear still mingles
 With the voices of whisp'ring trees;
Thy kiss on my cheek still tingles
 At each kiss of the summer breeze;
While dreams of the past are thronging
 For substance of shades in vain,
I am waiting, watching, and longing —
 Thou comest not back again.

Waiting and watching ever,
 Longing and lingering yet,
Leaves rustle and corn-stalks quiver,
 Winds murmur and waters fret;
No answer they bring, no greeting,
 No speech save that sad refrain,
Nor voice, save an echo repeating —
 He cometh not back again.

The Three Friends
(From the French)

The sword slew one in deadly strife;
　One perish'd by the bowl;
The third lies self-slain by the knife;
　For three the bells may toll —
I loved her better than my life,
　And better than my soul.

Aye, father! hast thou come at last?
　'Tis somewhat late to pray;
Life's crimson tides are ebbing fast,
　They drain my soul away;
Mine eyes with film are overcast,
　The lights are waning grey.

This curl from her bright head I shore,
　And this her hands gave mine;
See, one is stained with purple gore,
　And one with poison'd wine;
Give these to her when all is o'er —
　How serpent-like they twine!

We three were brethren in arms,
　And sworn companions we;
We held this motto, "Whoso harms
　The one shall harm the three!"
Till, matchless for her subtle charms,
　Beloved of each was she.

(These two were slain that I might kiss
　Her sweet mouth. I did well;
I said, "There is no greater bliss
　For those in heaven that dwell;"
I lost her; then I said, "There is
　No fiercer pang in hell!")

We have upheld each other's rights,
 Shared purse, and borrow'd blade;
Have stricken side by side in fights;
 And side by side have prayed
In churches. We were Christian knights,
 And she a Christian maid.

We met at sunrise, he and I,
 My comrade — 'twas agreed
The steel our quarrel first should try,
 The poison should succeed;
For two of three were doom'd to die,
 And one was doom'd to bleed.

We buckled to the doubtful fray,
 At first with some remorse;
But he who must be slain, or slay,
 Soon strikes with vengeful force.
He fell; I left him where he lay,
 Among the trampled gorse.

Did passion warp my heart and head
 To madness? And, if so,
Can madness palliate bloodshed? —
 It may be — I shall know
When God shall gather up the dead
 From where the four winds blow.

We met at sunset, he and I —
 My second comrade true;
Two cups with wine were brimming high,
 And one was drugg'd — we knew
Not which, nor sought we to descry;
 Our choice by lot we drew.

And there I sat with him to sup;
 I heard him blithely speak
Of by-gone days — the fatal cup
 Forgotten seem'd — his cheek
Was ruddy: father, raise me up,
 My voice is waxing weak.

We drank; his lips turned livid white,

His cheeks grew leaden ash;
He reel'd — I heard his temples smite
　The threshold with a crash!
And from his hand, in shivers bright,
　I saw the goblet flash.

The morrow dawn'd with fragrance rare,
　The May breeze, from the west,
Just fann'd the sleepy olives, where
　She heard and I confess'd;
My hair entangled with her hair,
　Her breast strained to my breast.

On the dread verge of endless gloom
　My soul recalls that hour;
Skies languishing with balm of bloom,
　And fields aflame with flower;
And slow caresses that consume,
　And kisses that devour.

Ah! now with storm the day seems rife,
　My dull ears catch the roll
Of thunder, and the far sea strife,
　On beach and bar and shoal —
I loved her better than my life,
　And better than my soul.

She fled! I cannot prove her guilt,
　Nor would I an I could;
See, life for life is fairly spilt!
　And blood is shed for blood;
Her white hands neither touched the hilt,
　Nor yet the potion brew'd.

Aye! turn me from the sickly south,
　Towards the gusty north;
The fruits of sin are dust and drouth,
　The end of crime is wrath —
The lips that pressed her rose-like mouth
　Are choked with blood-red froth.

Then dig the grave-pit deep and wide,
　Three graves thrown into one,

And lay three corpses side by side,
 And tell their tale to none;
But bring her back in all her pride
 To see what she hath done.

A Song of Autumn

"Where shall we go for our garlands glad
　At the falling of the year,
When the burnt-up banks are yellow and sad,
　When the boughs are yellow and sere?
Where are the old ones that once we had,
　And when are the new ones near?
What shall we do for our garlands glad
　At the falling of the year?"

"Child! can I tell where the garlands go?
　Can I say where the lost leaves veer
On the brown-burnt banks, when the wild winds blow,
　When they drift through the dead-wood drear?
Girl! when the garlands of next year glow,
　YOU may gather again, my dear —
But I go where the last year's lost leaves go
　At the falling of the year."

The Romance of Britomarte

As related by Sergeant Leigh on the night he got his captaincy at the Restoration.

I'll tell you a story; but pass the "jack",
  And let us make merry to-night, my men.
Aye, those were the days when my beard was black —
  I like to remember them now and then —
Then Miles was living, and Cuthbert there,
  On his lip was never a sign of down;
But I carry about some braided hair,
  That has not yet changed from the glossy brown
That it showed the day when I broke the heart
Of that bravest of destriers, "Britomarte".

Sir Hugh was slain (may his soul find grace!)
  In the fray that was neither lost nor won
At Edgehill — then to St. Hubert's Chase
  Lord Goring despatched a garrison —
But men and horses were ill to spare,
  And ere long the soldiers were shifted fast.
As for me, I never was quartered there
  Till Marston Moor had been lost; at last,
As luck would have it, alone, and late
In the night, I rode to the northern gate.

I thought, as I passed through the moonlit park,
  On the boyish days I used to spend
In the halls of the knight lying stiff and stark —
  Thought on his lady, my father's friend
(Mine, too, in spite of my sinister bar,
  But with that my story has naught to do) —
She died the winter before the war —
  Died giving birth to the baby Hugh.
He pass'd ere the green leaves clothed the bough,
And the orphan girl was the heiress now.

When I was a rude and a reckless boy,
 And she a brave and a beautiful child,
I was her page, her playmate, her toy —
 I have crown'd her hair with the field-flowers wild,
Cowslip and crow-foot and colt's-foot bright —
 I have carried her miles when the woods were wet,
I have read her romances of dame and knight;
 She was my princess, my pride, my pet,
There was then this proverb us twain between,
For the glory of God and of Gwendoline.

She had grown to a maiden wonderful fair,
 But for years I had scarcely seen her face.
Now, with troopers Holdsworth, Huntly, and Clare,
 Old Miles kept guard at St. Hubert's Chase,
And the chatelaine was a Mistress Ruth,
 Sir Hugh's half-sister, an ancient dame,
But a mettlesome soul had she forsooth,
 As she show'd when the time of her trial came.
I bore despatches to Miles and to her,
To warn them against the bands of Kerr.

And mine would have been a perilous ride
 With the rebel horsemen — we knew not where
They were scattered over that country side, —
 If it had not been for my brave brown mare.
She was iron-sinew'd and satin-skinn'd,
 Ribb'd like a drum and limb'd like a deer,
Fierce as the fire and fleet as the wind —
 There was nothing she couldn't climb or clear —
Rich lords had vex'd me, in vain, to part,
For their gold and silver, with Britomarte.

Next morn we muster'd scarce half a score,
 With the serving men, who were poorly arm'd —
Five soldiers, counting myself, no more,
 And a culverin, which might well have harm'd
Us, had we used it, but not our foes,
 When, with horses and foot, to our doors they came,
And a psalm-singer summon'd us (through his nose),
 And deliver'd — "This, in the people's name,
Unto whoso holdeth this fortress here,
Surrender! or bide the siege — John Kerr."

'Twas a mansion built in a style too new,
　A castle by courtesy, he lied
Who called it a fortress — yet, 'tis true,
　It had been indifferently fortified —
We were well provided with bolt and bar —
　And while I hurried to place our men,
Old Miles was call'd to a council of war
　With Mistress Ruth and with HER, and when
They had argued loudly and long, those three,
They sent, as a last resource, for me.

In the chair of state sat erect Dame Ruth;
　She had cast aside her embroidery;
She had been a beauty, they say, in her youth,
　There was much fierce fire in her bold black eye.
"Am I deceived in you both?" quoth she.
　"If one spark of her father's spirit lives
In this girl here — so, this Leigh, Ralph Leigh,
　Let us hear what counsel the springald gives."
Then I stammer'd, somewhat taken aback —
(Simon, you ale-swiller, pass the "jack").

The dame wax'd hotter — "Speak out, lad, say,
　Must we fall in that canting caitiff's power?
Shall we yield to a knave and a turncoat? Nay,
　I had liever leap from our topmost tower.
For a while we can surely await relief;
　Our walls are high and our doors are strong."
This Kerr was indeed a canting thief —
　I know not rightly, some private wrong
He had done Sir Hugh, but I know this much,
Traitor or turncoat, he suffer'd as such.

Quoth Miles — "Enough! your will shall be done;
　Relief may arrive by the merest chance,
But your house ere dusk will be lost and won;
　They have got three pieces of ordnance."
Then I cried, "Lord Guy, with four troops of horse,
　Even now is biding at Westbrooke town;
If a rider could break through the rebel force,
　He would bring relief ere the sun goes down;
Through the postern door could I make one dart,
I could baffle them all upon Britomarte."

Miles mutter'd "Madness!" Dame Ruth look'd grave,
  Said, "True, though we cannot keep one hour
The courtyard, no, nor the stables save,
  They will have to batter piecemeal the tower,
And thus — —" But suddenly she halted there.
  With a shining hand on my shoulder laid
Stood Gwendoline. She had left her chair,
  And, "Nay, if it needs must be done," she said,
"Ralph Leigh will gladly do it, I ween,
For the glory of God and of Gwendoline."

I had undertaken a heavier task
  For a lighter word. I saddled with care,
Nor cumber'd myself with corselet nor casque
  (Being loth to burden the brave brown mare).
Young Clare kept watch on the wall — he cried,
  "Now, haste, Ralph! this is the time to seize;
The rebels are round us on every side,
  But here they straggle by twos and threes."
Then out I led her, and up I sprung,
And the postern door on its hinges swung.

I had drawn this sword — you may draw it and feel,
  For this is the blade that I bore that day —
There's a notch even now on the long grey steel,
  A nick that has never been rasp'd away.
I bow'd my head and I buried my spurs,
  One bound brought the gliding green beneath;
I could tell by her back-flung, flatten'd ears,
  She had fairly taken the bit in her teeth —
(What, Jack, have you drain'd your namesake dry,
Left nothing to quench the thirst of a fly?)

These things are done, and are done with, lad,
  In far less time than your talker tells;
The sward with their hoof-strokes shook like mad,
  And rang with their carbines and petronels;
And they shouted, "Cross him and cut him off,"
  "Surround him," "Seize him," "Capture the clown,
Or kill him," "Shall he escape to scoff
  In your faces?" "Shoot him or cut him down."
And their bullets whistled on every side;
Many were near us and more were wide.

Not a bullet told upon Britomarte;
 Suddenly snorting, she launched along;
So the osprey dives where the seagulls dart,
 So the falcon swoops where the kestrels throng.
And full in my front one pistol flash'd,
 And right in my path their sergeant got.
How are jack-boots jarr'd, how are stirrups clash'd,
 While the mare like a meteor past him shot;
But I clove his skull with a backstroke clean,
For the glory of God and of Gwendoline.

And as one whom the fierce wind storms in the face,
 With spikes of hail and with splinters of rain,
I, while we fled through St. Hubert's Chase,
 Bent till my cheek was amongst her mane.
To the north, full a league of the deer-park lay,
 Smooth, springy turf, and she fairly flew,
And the sound of their hoof-strokes died away,
 And their far shots faint in the distance grew.
Loudly I laughed, having won the start,
At the folly of following Britomarte.

They had posted a guard at the northern gate —
 Some dozen of pikemen and musketeers.
To the tall park palings I turn'd her straight;
 She veer'd in her flight as the swallow veers.
And some blew matches and some drew swords,
 And one of them wildly hurl'd his pike,
But she clear'd by inches the oaken boards,
 And she carried me yards beyond the dyke;
Then gaily over the long green down
We gallop'd, heading for Westbrooke town.

The green down slopes to the great grey moor,
 The grey moor sinks to the gleaming Skelt —
Sudden and sullen, and swift and sure,
 The whirling water was round my belt.
She breasted the bank with a savage snort,
 And a backward glance of her bloodshot eye,
And "Our Lady of Andover's" flash'd like thought,
 And flitted St. Agatha's nunnery,
And the firs at "The Ferngrove" fled on the right,
And "Falconer's Tower" on the left took flight.

And over "The Ravenswold" we raced —
We rounded the hill by "The Hermit's Well" —
We burst on the Westbrooke Bridge — "What haste?
What errand?" shouted the sentinel.
"To Beelzebub with the Brewer's knave!"
"Carolus Rex and he of the Rhine!"
Galloping past him, I got and gave
 In the gallop password and countersign,
All soak'd with water and soil'd with mud,
With the sleeve of my jerkin half drench'd in blood.

Now, Heaven be praised that I found him there —
Lord Guy. He said, having heard my tale,
"Leigh, let my own man look to your mare,
 Rest and recruit with our wine and ale;
But first must our surgeon attend to you;
 You are somewhat shrewdly stricken, no doubt."
Then he snatched a horn from the wall and blew,
 Making "Boot and Saddle" ring sharply out.
"Have I done good service this day?" quoth I.
"Then I will ride back in your troop, Lord Guy."

In the street I heard how the trumpets peal'd,
 And I caught the gleam of a morion
From the window — then to the door I reel'd;
I had lost more blood than I reckon'd upon;
He eyed me calmly with keen grey eyes —
 Stern grey eyes of a steel-blue grey —
Said, "The wilful man can never be wise,
 Nathless, the wilful must have his way,"
And he pour'd from a flagon some fiery wine;
I drain'd it, and straightway strength was mine.

* * * * *

I was with them all the way on the brown —
 "Guy to the rescue!" "God and the king!"
We were just in time, for the doors were down;
 And didn't our sword-blades rasp and ring,
And didn't we hew and didn't we hack?
 The sport scarce lasted minutes ten —
(Aye, those were the days when my beard was black;
 I like to remember them now and then).

Though they fought like fiends, we were four to one,
And we captured those that refused to run.

We have not forgotten it, Cuthbert, boy!
 That supper scene when the lamps were lit;
How the women (some of them) sobb'd for joy,
 How the soldiers drank the deeper for it;
How the dame did honours, and Gwendoline,
 How grandly she glided into the hall,
How she stoop'd with the grace of a girlish queen,
 And kiss'd me gravely before them all;
And the stern Lord Guy, how gaily he laugh'd,
Till more of his cup was spilt than quaff'd.

Brown Britomarte lay dead in her straw
 Next morn — we buried her — brave old girl!
John Kerr, we tried him by martial law,
 And we twisted some hemp for the trait'rous churl;
And she — I met her alone — said she,
 "You have risk'd your life, you have lost your mare,
And what can I give in return, Ralph Leigh?"
 I replied, "One braid of that bright brown hair."
And with that she bow'd her beautiful head,
"You can take as much as you choose," she said.

And I took it — it may be, more than enough —
 And I shore it rudely, close to the roots.
The wine or wounds may have made me rough,
 And men at the bottom are merely brutes.
Three weeks I slept at St. Hubert's Chase;
 When I woke from the fever of wounds and wine,
I could scarce believe that the ghastly face
 That the glass reflected was really mine.
I sought the hall — where a wedding HAD BEEN —
The wedding of Guy and of Gwendoline.

The romance of a grizzled old trooper's life
 May make you laugh in your sleeves: laugh out,
Lads; we have most of us seen some strife;
 We have all of us had some sport, no doubt.
I have won some honour and gain'd some gold,
 Now that our king returns to his own;
If the pulses beat slow, if the blood runs cold,

And if friends have faded and loves have flown,
Then the greater reason is ours to drink,
And the more we swallow the less we shall think.

At the battle of Naseby, Miles was slain,
 And Huntly sank from his wounds that week;
We left young Clare upon Worcester plain —
 How the "Ironside" gash'd his girlish cheek.
Aye, strut, and swagger, and ruffle anew,
 Gay gallants, now that the war is done!
They fought like fiends (give the fiend his due) —
We fought like fops, it was thus they won.
Holdsworth is living for aught I know,
At least he was living two years ago,

And Guy — Lord Guy — so stately and stern,
 He is changed, I met him at Winchester;
He has grown quite gloomy and taciturn.
 Gwendoline! — why do you ask for her?
Died as her mother had died before —
 Died giving birth to the baby Guy!
Did my voice shake? Then am I fool the more.
 Sooner or later we all must die;
But, at least, let us live while we live to-night.
The DAYS may be dark, but the LAMPS are bright.

For to me the sunlight seems worn and wan:
 The sun, he is losing his splendour now —
He can never shine as of old he shone
 On her glorious hair and glittering brow.
Ah! those DAYS THAT WERE, when my beard was black,
 NOW I have only the NIGHTS THAT ARE.
What, landlord, ho! bring in haste burnt sack,
 And a flask of your fiercest usquebaugh.
You, Cuthbert! surely you know by heart
The story of HER and of Britomarte.

Laudamus

The Lord shall slay or the Lord shall save!
 He is righteous whether He save or slay —
Brother, give thanks for the gifts He gave,
 Though the gifts He gave He hath taken away.
Shall we strive for that which is nothing? Nay.
Shall we hate each other for that which fled?
 She is but a marvel of modelled clay,
And the smooth, clear white, and the soft, pure red,
 That we coveted, shall endure no day.

Was it wise or well that I hated you
 For the fruit that hung too high on the tree?
For the blossom out of our reach that grew,
 Was it well or wise that you hated me? —
My hate has flown, and your hate shall flee.
Let us veil our faces like children chid —
 Can that violet orb we swore by see
Through that violet-vein'd, transparent lid? —
 Now the Lord forbid that this strife should be.

Would you knit the forehead or clench the fist,
 For the curls that never were well caress'd —
For the red that never was fairly kiss'd —
 For the white that never was fondly press'd?
Shall we nourish wrath while she lies at rest
Between us? Surely our wrath shall cease.
 We would fain know better — the Lord knows best —
Is there peace between us? Yea, there is peace,
 In the soul's release she at least is blest.

Let us thank the Lord for His bounties all,
 For the brave old days of pleasure and pain,
When the world for both of us seem'd too small —
 Though the love was void and the hate was vain —
 Though the word was bitter between us twain,
And the bitter word was kin to the blow,

For her gloss and ripple of rich gold rain,
For her velvet crimson and satin snow —
Though we never shall know the old days again.

The Lord! — His mercy is great, men say;
 His wrath, men say, is a burning brand —
Let us praise Him whether He save or slay,
 And above her body let hand join hand.
 We shall meet, my friend, in the spirit land —
Will our strife renew? Nay, I dare not trust,
 For the grim, great gulf that cannot be spann'd
Will divide us from her. The Lord is just,
 She shall not be thrust where our spirits stand.

A Basket of Flowers

from Dawn to Dusk

Dawn

On skies still and starlit
 White lustres take hold,
And grey flushes scarlet,
 And red flashes gold.
And sun-glories cover
The rose shed above her,
Like lover and lover
 They flame and unfold.

* * * * *

Still bloom in the garden
 Green grass-plot, fresh lawn,
Though pasture lands harden
 And drought fissures yawn.
While leaves not a few fall,
Let rose leaves for you fall,
Leaves pearl-strung with dew-fall,
 And gold shot with dawn.

Does the grass-plot remember
 The fall of your feet
In autumn's red ember,
 When drought leagues with heat,
When the last of the roses
Despairingly closes
In the lull that reposes
 Ere storm winds wax fleet?

Love's melodies languish
 In "Chastelard's" strain,

And "Abelard's" anguish
 Is love's pleasant pain!
And "Sappho" rehearses
Love's blessings and curses
In passionate verses
 Again and again.

And I! — I have heard of
 All these long ago,
Yet never one word of
 Their song-lore I know;
Not under my finger
In songs of the singer
Love's litanies linger,
 Love's rhapsodies flow.

Fresh flowers in a basket —
 An offering to you —
Though you did not ask it,
 Unbidden I strew;
With heat and drought striving,
Some blossoms still living
May render thanksgiving
 For dawn and for dew.

The garlands I gather,
 The rhymes I string fast,
Are hurriedly rather
 Than heedlessly cast.
Yon tree's shady awning
Is short'ning, and warning
Far spent is the morning,
 And I must ride fast.

Songs empty, yet airy,
 I've striven to write,
For failure, dear Mary!
 Forgive me — Good-night!
Songs and flowers may beset you,
I can only regret you,
While the soil where I met you
 Recedes from my sight.

For the sake of past hours,
 For the love of old times,
Take "A Basket of Flowers",
 And a bundle of rhymes;
Though all the bloom perish
E'en YOUR hand can cherish,
While churlish and bearish
 The verse-jingle chimes.

And Eastward by Nor'ward
 Looms sadly MY track,
And I must ride forward,
 And still I look back, —
Look back — ah, how vainly!
For while I see plainly,
My hands on the reins lie
 Uncertain and slack.

The warm wind breathes strong breath,
 The dust dims mine eye,
And I draw one long breath,
 And stifle one sigh.
Green slopes, softly shaded,
Have flitted and faded —
My dreams flit as they did —
 Good-night! — and — Good-bye!

* * * * *

Dusk

Lost rose! end my story!
 Dead core and dry husk —
Departed thy glory
 And tainted thy musk.
Night spreads her dark limbs on
The face of the dim sun,
So flame fades to crimson
 And crimson to dusk.

A Fragment

They say that poison-sprinkled flowers
 Are sweeter in perfume
Than when, untouched by deadly dew,
 They glowed in early bloom.

They say that men condemned to die
 Have quaffed the sweetened wine
With higher relish than the juice
 Of the untampered vine.

They say that in the witch's song,
 Though rude and harsh it be,
There blends a wild, mysterious strain
 Of weirdest melody.

And I believe the devil's voice
 Sinks deeper in our ear
Than any whisper sent from Heaven,
 However sweet and clear.

[End of Bush Ballads.]

Miscellaneous Poems

To My Sister

Lines written by the late A. L. Gordon
On 4th August, 1853, Being three days before he sailed for Australia.

Across the trackless seas I go,
  No matter when or where,
And few my future lot will know,
  And fewer still will care.
My hopes are gone, my time is spent,
  I little heed their loss,
And if I cannot feel content,
  I cannot feel remorse.

My parents bid me cross the flood,
  My kindred frowned at me;
They say I have belied my blood,
  And stained my pedigree.
But I must turn from those who chide,
  And laugh at those who frown;
I cannot quench my stubborn pride,
  Nor keep my spirits down.

I once had talents fit to win
  Success in life's career,
And if I chose a part of sin,
  My choice has cost me dear.
But those who brand me with disgrace
  Will scarcely dare to say
They spoke the taunt before my face,
  And went unscathed away.

My friends will miss a comrade's face,
  And pledge me on the seas,
Who shared the wine-cup or the chase,

Or follies worse than these.
A careless smile, a parting glass,
  A hand that waves adieu,
And from my sight they soon will pass,
  And from my memory too.

I loved a girl not long ago,
  And, till my suit was told,
I thought her breast as fair as snow,
  'Twas very near as cold;
And yet I spoke, with feelings more
  Of recklessness than pain,
Those words I never spoke before,
  Nor never shall again.

Her cheek grew pale, in her dark eye
  I saw the tear-drop shine;
Her red lips faltered in reply,
  And then were pressed to mine.
A quick pulsation of the heart!
  A flutter of the breath!
A smothered sob — and thus we part,
  To meet no more till death.

And yet I may at times recall
  Her memory with a sigh;
At times for me the tears may fall
  And dim her sparkling eye.
But absent friends are soon forgot,
  And in a year or less
'Twill doubtless be another's lot
  Those very lips to press!

With adverse fate we best can cope
  When all we prize has fled;
And where there's little left to hope,
  There's little left to dread!
Oh, time glides ever quickly by!
  Destroying all that's dear;
On earth there's little worth a sigh,
  And nothing worth a tear!

What fears have I? What hopes in life?

What joys can I command?
A few short years of toil and strife
  In a strange and distant land!
When green grass sprouts above this clay
  (And that might be ere long),
Some friends may read these lines and say,
  The world has judged him wrong.

There is a spot not far away
  Where my young sister sleeps,
Who seems alive but yesterday,
  So fresh her memory keeps;
For we have played in childhood there
  Beneath the hawthorn's bough,
And bent our knee in childish prayer
  I cannot utter now!

Of late so reckless and so wild,
  That spot recalls to me
That I was once a laughing child,
  As innocent as she;
And there, while August's wild flow'rs wave,
  I wandered all alone,
Strewed blossoms on her little grave,
  And knelt beside the stone.

I seem to have a load to bear,
  A heavy, choking grief;
Could I have forced a single tear
  I might have felt relief.
I think my hot and restless heart
  Has scorched the channels dry,
From which those sighs of sorrow start
  To moisten cheek and eye.

Sister, farewell! farewell once more
  To every youthful tie!
Friends! parents! kinsmen! native shore!
  To each and all good-bye!
And thoughts which for the moment seem
  To bind me with a spell,
Ambitious hope! love's boyish dream!
  To you a last farewell!

"The Old Leaven"
A Dialogue

Mark:
So, Maurice, you sail to-morrow, you say?
  And you may or may not return?
Be sociable, man! for once in a way,
  Unless you're too old to learn.
The shadows are cool by the water side
  Where the willows grow by the pond,
And the yellow laburnum's drooping pride
  Sheds a golden gleam beyond.
For the blended tints of the summer flowers,
  For the scents of the summer air,
For all nature's charms in this world of ours,
  'Tis little or naught you care.
Yet I know for certain you haven't stirred
  Since noon from your chosen spot;
And you've hardly spoken a single word —
  Are you tired, or cross, or what?
You're fretting about those shares you bought,
  They were to have gone up fast;
But I heard how they fell to nothing — in short,
  They were given away at last.

Maurice:
No, Mark, I'm not so easily cross'd;
  'Tis true that I've had a run
Of bad luck lately; indeed, I've lost;
  Well! somebody else has won.

Mark:
The glass has fallen, perhaps you fear
  A return of your ancient stitch —
That souvenir of the Lady's Mere,
  Park palings and double ditch.

Maurice:
You're wrong. I'm not in the least afraid
　Of that. If the truth be told,
When the stiffness visits my shoulder-blade,
　I think on the days of old;
It recalls the rush of the freshening wind,
　The strain of the chestnut springing,
And the rolling thunder of hoofs behind,
　Like the Rataplan chorus ringing.

Mark:
Are you bound to borrow, or loth to lend?
　Have you purchased another screw?
Or backed a bill for another friend?
　Or had a bad night at loo?

Maurice:
Not one of those, you're all in the dark,
　If you choose you can guess again;
But you'd better give over guessing, Mark,
　It's only labour in vain.

Mark:
I'll try once more; does it plague you still,
　That trifle of lead you carry?
A guest that lingers against your will,
　Unwelcome, yet bound to tarry.

Maurice:
Not so! That burden I'm used to bear,
　'Tis seldom it gives me trouble;
And to earn it as I did then and there,
　I'd carry a dead weight double.
A shock like that for a splintered rib
　Can a thousand-fold repay —
As the swallow skims through the spider's web,
　We rode through their ranks that day!

Mark:
Come, Maurice, you sha'n't escape me so!
　I'll hazard another guess:
That girl that jilted you long ago,
　You're thinking of her, confess!

Maurice:
Tho' the blue lake flush'd with a rosy light,
 Reflected from yonder sky,
Might conjure a vision of Aphrodite
 To a poet's or painter's eye;
Tho' the golden drop, with its drooping curl,
 Between the water and wood,
Hangs down like the tress of a wayward girl
 In her dreamy maidenhood:
Such boyish fancies seem out of date
 To one half inclined to censure
Their folly, and yet — your shaft flew straight,
 Though you drew your bow at a venture.
I saw my lady the other night
 In the crowded opera hall,
When the boxes sparkled with faces bright,
 I knew her amongst them all.
Tho' little for these things now I reck,
 I singled her from the throng
By the queenly curves of her head and neck,
 By the droop of her eyelash long.
Oh! passionless, placid, and calm, and cold,
 Does the fire still lurk within
That lit her magnificent eyes of old,
 And coloured her marble skin?
For a weary look on the proud face hung,
 While the music clash'd and swell'd,
And the restless child to the silk skirt clung
 Unnoticed tho' unrepelled.
They've paled, those rosebud lips that I kist,
 That slim waist has thickened rather,
And the cub has the sprawling mutton fist,
 And the great splay foot of the father.
May the blight — —

Mark: Hold hard there, Maurice, my son,
 Let her rest, since her spell is broken;
We can neither recall deeds rashly done,
 Nor retract words hastily spoken.

Maurice:
Time was when to pleasure her girlish whim,
 In my blind infatuation,

I've freely endangered life and limb;
　Aye, perilled my soul's salvation.

Mark:
With the best intentions we all must work
　But little good and much harm;
Be a Christian for once, not a Pagan Turk,
　Nursing wrath and keeping it warm.

Maurice:
If our best intentions pave the way
　To a place that is somewhat hot,
Can our worst intentions lead us, say,
　To a still more sultry spot?

Mark:
'Tis said that charity makes amends
　For a multitude of transgressions.

Maurice:
But our perjured loves and our faithless friends
　Are entitled to no concessions.

Mark:
Old man, these many years side by side
　Our parallel paths have lain;
Now, in life's long journey, diverging wide,
　They can scarcely unite again;
And tho', from all that I've seen and heard,
　You're prone to chafe and to fret
At the least restraint, not one angry word
　Have we two exchanged as yet.
We've shared our peril, we've shared our sport,
　Our sunshine and gloomy weather,
Feasted and flirted, and fenced and fought,
　Struggled and toiled together;
In happier moments lighter of heart,
　Stouter of heart in sorrow;
We've met and we've parted, and now we part
　For ever, perchance, to-morrow.
She's a matron now; when you knew her first
　She was but a child, and your hate,
Fostered and cherished, nourished and nursed,

Will it never evaporate?
Your grievance is known to yourself alone,
　But, Maurice, I say, for shame,
If in ten long years you haven't outgrown
　Ill-will to an ancient flame.

Maurice:
Well, Mark, you're right; if I spoke in spite,
　Let the shame and the blame be mine;
At the risk of a headache we'll drain this night
　Her health in a flask of wine;
For a castle in Spain, tho' it never was built;
　For a dream, tho' it never came true;
For a cup, just tasted, tho' rudely spilt,
　At least she can hold me due.
Those hours of pleasure she dealt of yore,
　As well as those hours of pain,
I ween they would flit as they flitted before,
　If I had them over again.
Against her no word from my lips shall pass,
　Betraying the grudge I've cherished,
Till the sand runs down in my hour-glass,
　And the gift of my speech has perished.
Say! why is the spirit of peace so weak,
　And the spirit of wrath so strong,
That the right we must steadily search and seek,
　Tho' we readily find the wrong?

Mark:
Our parents of old entailed the curse
　Which must to our children cling;
Let us hope, at least, that we're not much worse
　Than the founder from whom we spring.
Fit sire was he of a selfish race,
　Who first to temptation yielded,
Then to mend his case tried to heap disgrace
　On the woman he should have shielded.
Say! comrade mine, the forbidden fruit
　We'd have plucked, that I well believe,
But I trust we'd rather have suffered mute
　Than have laid the blame upon Eve.

Maurice (yawning):
Who knows? not I; I can hardly vouch
 For the truth of what little I see;
And now, if you've any weed in your pouch,
 Just hand it over to me.

An Exile's Farewell

The ocean heaves around us still
  With long and measured swell,
The autumn gales our canvas fill,
  Our ship rides smooth and well.
The broad Atlantic's bed of foam
  Still breaks against our prow;
I shed no tears at quitting home,
  Nor will I shed them now!

Against the bulwarks on the poop
  I lean, and watch the sun
Behind the red horizon stoop —
  His race is nearly run.
Those waves will never quench his light,
  O'er which they seem to close,
To-morrow he will rise as bright
  As he this morning rose.

How brightly gleams the orb of day
  Across the trackless sea!
How lightly dance the waves that play
  Like dolphins in our lee!
The restless waters seem to say,
  In smothered tones to me,
How many thousand miles away
  My native land must be!

Speak, Ocean! is my Home the same
  Now all is new to me? —
The tropic sky's resplendent flame,
  The vast expanse of sea?
Does all around her, yet unchanged,
  The well-known aspect wear?
Oh! can the leagues that I have ranged
  Have made no difference there?

How vivid Recollection's hand
  Recalls the scene once more!
I see the same tall poplars stand
  Beside the garden door;
I see the bird-cage hanging still;
  And where my sister set
The flowers in the window-sill —
  Can they be living yet?

Let woman's nature cherish grief,
  I rarely heave a sigh
Before emotion takes relief
  In listless apathy;
While from my pipe the vapours curl
  Towards the evening sky,
And 'neath my feet the billows whirl
  In dull monotony!

The sky still wears the crimson streak
  Of Sol's departing ray,
Some briny drops are on my cheek,
  'Tis but the salt sea spray!
Then let our barque the ocean roam,
  Our keel the billows plough;
I shed no tears at quitting home,
  Nor will I shed them now!

"Early Adieux"

Adieu to kindred hearts and home,
 To pleasure, joy, and mirth,
A fitter foot than mine to roam
 Could scarcely tread the earth;
For they are now so few indeed
 (Not more than three in all),
Who e'er will think of me or heed
 What fate may me befall.

For I through pleasure's paths have run
 My headlong goal to win,
Nor pleasure's snares have cared to shun
 When pleasure sweetened sin.
Let those who will their failings mask,
 To mine I frankly own;
But for them pardon will I ask
 Of none — save Heaven alone.

From carping friends I turn aside;
 At foes defiance frown;
Yet time may tame my stubborn pride,
 And break my spirit down.
Still, if to error I incline,
 Truth whispers comfort strong,
That never reckless act of mine
 E'er worked a comrade wrong.

My mother is a stately dame,
 Who oft would chide with me;
She saith my riot bringeth shame,
 And stains my pedigree.
I'd reck not what my friends might know,
 Or what the world might say,
Did I but think some tears would flow
 When I am far away.

Perchance my mother will recall
 My mem'ry with a sigh;
My gentle sister's tears may fall,
 And dim her laughing eye;
Perhaps a loving thought may gleam,
 And fringe its saddened ray,
When, like a nightmare's troubled dream,
 I, outcast, pass away.

Then once again farewell to those
 Whoe'er for me have sighed;
For pleasures melt away like snows,
 And hopes like shadows glide.
Adieu, my mother! if no more
 Thy son's face thou may'st see,
At least those many cares are o'er
 So ofttimes caused by me.

My lot is fixed! The die is cast!
 For me home hath no joy!
Oh, pardon then all follies past,
 And bless your wayward boy!
And thou, from whom for aye to part
 Grieves more than tongue can tell,
May Heaven preserve thy guileless heart,
 Sweet sister, fare thee well!

Thou, too, whose loving-kindness makes
 My resolution less,
While from the bitter past it takes
 One half its bitterness,
If e'er you held my mem'ry dear,
 Grant this request, I pray —
Give to that mem'ry one bright tear,
 And let it pass away.

A Hunting Song

Here's a health to every sportsman, be he stableman or lord,
If his heart be true, I care not what his pocket may afford;
And may he ever pleasantly each gallant sport pursue,
If he takes his liquor fairly, and his fences fairly, too.

He cares not for the bubbles of Fortune's fickle tide,
Who like Bendigo can battle, and like Olliver can ride.
He laughs at those who caution, at those who chide he'll frown,
As he clears a five-foot paling, or he knocks a peeler down.

The dull, cold world may blame us, boys! but what care we the while,
If coral lips will cheer us, and bright eyes on us smile?
For beauty's fond caresses can most tenderly repay
The weariness and trouble of many an anxious day.

Then fill your glass, and drain it, too, with all your heart and soul,
To the best of sports — The Fox-hunt, The Fair Ones, and The Bowl,
To a stout heart in adversity through every ill to steer,
And when Fortune smiles a score of friends like those around us here.

To a Proud Beauty

"A Valentine"

Though I have loved you well, I ween,
 And you, too, fancied me,
Your heart hath too divided been
 A constant heart to be.
And like the gay and youthful knight,
 Who loved and rode away,
Your fleeting fancy takes a flight
 With every fleeting day.

So let it be as you propose,
 Tho' hard the struggle be;
'Tis fitter far — that goodness knows! —
 Since we cannot agree.
Let's quarrel once for all, my sweet,
 Forget the past — and then
I'll kiss each pretty girl I meet,
 While you'll flirt with the men.

Thick-headed Thoughts

No. I

I've something of the bull-dog in my breed,
 The spaniel is developed somewhat less;
While life is in me I can fight and bleed,
 But never the chastising hand caress.
You say the stroke was well intended. "True."
 You mention "It was meant to do me good."
"That may be." "You deserve it." "Granted, too."
 "Then take it kindly." "No — I never could."

* * * * *

How many a resolution to amend
 Is made, and broken, as the years run round!
And how can others on your word depend,
 When faithless to ourselves we're often found?
I've often swore — "Henceforward I'll reform,
 And bid my vices, follies, all take wing."
To keep my promise, 'mid temptation's storm,
 I've always found was quite another thing.

* * * * *

I saw a donkey going down the road
 The other day; a boy was on his back,
Who on the long-eared quadruped bestowed,
 With a stout cudgel, many a hearty thwack;
But lazier and lazier grew the beast,
 Until he dwindled to a step so slow
That I felt sure 'twould take him, at the least,
 Full half-an-hour one blessed mile to go.

Soliloquising on this state of things,
 "That moke's like me," I muttered, with a sigh;

"He might go faster if he'd got some wings,
  But Nature's made him better off than I;
For though I've all his obstinacy — aye! all —
  His sullen spirit, and his dogged ways,
I've not one particle, however small,
  Of that praiseworthy patience he displays."

No. II

A man is independent of the world,
  And little recks of strife or angry brawl,
If 'gainst a host his banner be unfurled,
  Be his heart stout, it matters not at all.
With woman 'tis not so; for she seems hurled
  From hand to hand, as is a tennis ball.
How queer that such a difference should be
Between a human he and human she.

No. III

'Tis a wicked world we live in;
  Wrong in reason, wrong in rhyme;
But no matter: we'll not give in
  While we still can come to time.

Strength's a shadow; Hope is madness,
  Love, delusion; Friendship, sham;
Pleasure fades away to sadness,
  None of these are worth a d— —n.

There is naught on earth to please us;
  All things at the crisis fail.
Friends desert us, bailiffs tease us —
  (To such foes we give leg-bail).

But a stout heart still maintaining,
  Quells the ills we all must meet,
And a spirit fear disdaining
  Lays our troubles at our feet.

So we'll ne'er surrender tamely
 To the ills that throng us fast.
If we must die, let's die gamely;
 Luck may take a turn at last.

[End of Miscellaneous Poems.]

Ashtaroth: A Dramatic Lyric

Dramatis Personae

HUGO, a Norman Baron and a Scholar.
ERIC, a friend of Hugo's.
THURSTON, |
EUSTACE, |
RALPH, | Followers of Hugo.
HENRY, a Page.
LUKE, |
HUBERT, | Monks living in a Norman Chapel.
BASIL, Abbot of a Convent on the Rhine.
CYRIL, a Monk of the same Convent.
OSRIC, a Norwegian Adventurer, and formerly a Corsair.
RUDOLPH, an Outlawed Count, and the Captain of a Band of Robbers.
DAGOBERT, the Captain of some predatory Soldiers called "Free Lances".
HAROLD, a Danish Knight.
ORION.
THORA, |
AGATHA, |
ELSPETH, a Nurse of Thora's, |
URSULA, Abbess of the Convent on the Rhine, |
NUNS, etc. | Women.

Men-at-arms, Soldiers, and Robbers; Monks, Friars, and Churchmen, Spirits, etc.

Ashtaroth: A Dramatic Lyric

SCENE — A Castle in Normandy.

A Study in a Tower; HUGO seated at a table covered with maps and charts of the heavens, astronomical instruments, books, manuscripts, &c.

Enter HENRY, a Page.

Hugo:
Well, boy, what is it?

Henry: The feast is spread.

Hugo:
 Why tarry the guests for me?
Let Eric sit at the table's head;
 Alone I desire to be.   [Henry goes out.]
What share have I at their festive board?
 Their mirth I can only mar;
To me no pleasure their cups afford,
 Their songs on my silence jar.
With an aching eye and a throbbing brain,
 And yet with a hopeful heart,
I must toil and strain with the planets again
 When the rays of the sun depart;
He who must needs with the topers tope,
 And the feasters feast in the hall,
How can he hope with a matter to cope
 That is immaterial?

Orion:
He who his appetite stints and curbs,
 Shut up in the northern wing,
With his rye-bread flavoured with bitter herbs,
 And his draught from the tasteless spring,

Good sooth, he is but a sorry clown.
 There are some good things upon earth —
Pleasure and power and fair renown,
 And wisdom of worldly worth!
There is wisdom in follies that charm the sense,
 In follies that light the eyes,
But the folly to wisdom that makes pretence
 Is alone by the fool termed wise.

Hugo:
Thy speech, Orion, is somewhat rude;
 Perchance, having jeer'd and scoff'd
To thy fill, thou wilt curb thy jeering mood;
 I wot thou hast served me oft.
This plan of the skies seems fairly traced;
 What errors canst thou detect?

Orion:
Nay, the constellations are misplaced,
 And the satellites incorrect;
Leave the plan to me; you have time to seek
 An hour of needful rest,
The night is young and the planets are weak;
 See, the sun still reddens the west.

Hugo:
I fear I shall sleep too long.

Orion: If you do
 It matters not much; the sky
Is cloudy, the stars will be faint and few;
 Now, list to my lullaby.
          [Hugo reclines on a couch.]
(Sings.)
Still the darkling skies are red,
 Though the day-god's course is run;
Heavenly night-lamps overhead
 Flash and twinkle one by one.
Idle dreamer — earth-born elf!
 Vainly grasping heavenly things,
Wherefore weariest thou thyself
 With thy vain imaginings?

From the tree of knowledge first,
  Since his parents pluck'd the fruit,
Man, with partial knowledge curs'd,
  Of the tree still seeks the root;
Musty volumes crowd thy shelf —
  Which of these true knowledge brings?
Wherefore weariest thou thyself
  With thy vain imaginings?

Will the stars from heaven descend?
  Can the earth-worm soar and rise?
Can the mortal comprehend
  Heaven's own hallow'd mysteries?
Greed and glory, power and pelf —
  These are won by clowns and kings;
Wherefore weariest thou thyself
  With thy vain imaginings?

Sow and reap, and toil and spin;
  Eat and drink, and dream and die;
Man may strive, yet never win,
  And I laugh the while and cry —
Idle dreamer, earth-born elf!
  Vainly grasping heavenly things,
Wherefore weariest thou thyself
  With thy vain imaginings?

He sleeps, and his sleep appears serene,
  Whatever dreams it has brought him —
         [Looks at the plans.]
If he knows what those hieroglyphics mean,
  He's wiser than one who taught him.
Why does he number the Pole-star thus?
  Or the Pleiades why combine?
And what is he doing with Sirius,
  In the devil's name or in mine?
Man thinks, discarding the beaten track,
  That the sins of his youth are slain,
When he seeks fresh sins, but he soon comes back
  To his old pet sins again.

SCENE — The Same.

HUGO waking, ORION seated near him. Daybreak.

Hugo:
Oh, weary spirit! oh, cloudy eyes!
  Oh, heavy and misty brain!
Yon riddle that lies 'twixt earth and skies,
  Ye seek to explore in vain!
See, the east is grey; put those scrolls away,
  And hide them far from my sight;
I will toil and study no more by day,
  I will watch no longer by night;
I have labour'd and long'd, and now I seem
  No nearer the mystic goal;
Orion, I fain would devise some scheme
  To quiet this restless soul;
To distant climes I would fain depart —
  I would travel by sea or land.

Orion:
Nay, I warn'd you of this, "Short life, long art",
  The proverb, though stale, will stand;
Full many a sage from youth to age
  Has toil'd to obtain what you
Would master at once. In a pilgrimage,
  Forsooth, there is nothing new;
Though virtue, I ween, in change of scene,
  And vigour in change of air,
Will always be, and has always been,
  And travel is a tonic rare.
Still, the restless, discontented mood
  For the time alone is eased;
It will soon return with hunger renew'd,
  And appetite unappeased.
Nathless I could teach a shorter plan
  To win that wisdom you crave,
That lore that is seldom attain'd by man
  From the cradle down to the grave.

Hugo:
Such lore I had rather do without,

It hath nothing mystic nor awful
In my eye. Nay, I despise and doubt
 The arts that are term'd unlawful;
'Twixt science and magic the line lies plain,
 I shall never wittingly pass it;
There is now no compact between us twain.

Orion: But an understanding tacit.
You have prospered much since the day we met;
 You were then a landless knight;
You now have honour and wealth, and yet
 I never can serve you right.

Hugo:
Enough; we will start this very day,
 Thurston, Eric, and I,
And the baffled visions will pass away,
 And the restless fires will die.

Orion:
Till the fuel expires that feeds those fires
 They smoulder and live unspent;
Give a mortal all that his heart desires,
 He is less than ever content.

SCENE — A Cliff on the Breton Coast, Overhanging the Sea.

HUGO.

Hugo:
Down drops the red sun; through the gloaming
 They burst — raging waves of the sea,
Foaming out their own shame — ever foaming
 Their leprosy up with fierce glee;
Flung back from the stone, snowy fountains
 Of feathery flakes, scarcely flag
Where, shock after shock, the green mountains
 Explode on the iron-grey crag.

The salt spray with ceaseless commotion
 Leaps round me. I sit on the verge

Of the cliff — 'twixt the earth and the ocean —
　With feet overhanging the surge.
In thy grandeur, oh, sea! we acknowledge,
　In thy fairness, oh, earth! we confess,
Hidden truths that are taught in no college,
　Hidden songs that no parchments express.

Were they wise in their own generations,
　Those sages and sagas of old?
They have pass'd; o'er their names and their nations
　Time's billows have silently roll'd;
They have pass'd, leaving little to their children,
　Save histories of a truth far from strict;
Or theories more vague and bewildering,
　Since three out of four contradict.

Lost labour! vain bookworms have sat in
　The halls of dull pedants who teach
Strange tongues, the dead lore of the Latin,
　The scroll that is god-like and Greek:
Have wasted life's springtide in learning
　Things long ago learnt all in vain;
They are slow, very slow, in discerning
　That book lore and wisdom are twain.

Pale shades of a creed that was mythic,
　By time or by truth overcome,
Your Delphian temples and Pythic
　Are ruins deserted and dumb;
Your Muses are hush'd, and your Graces
　Are bruised and defaced; and your gods,
Enshrin'd and enthron'd in high places
　No longer, are powerless as clods;

By forest and streamlet, where glisten'd
　Fair feet of the Naiads that skimm'd
The shallows; where the Oreads listen'd,
　Rose-lipp'd, amber-hair'd, marble-limb'd,
No lithe forms disport in the river,
　No sweet faces peer through the boughs,
Elms and beeches wave silent for ever,
　Ever silent the bright water flows.

(Were they duller or wiser than we are,
  Those heathens of old? Who shall say?
Worse or better? Thy wisdom, O "Thea
  Glaucopis", was wise in thy day;
And the false gods alluring to evil,
  That sway'd reckless votaries then,
Were slain to no purpose; they revel
  Re-crowned in the hearts of us men.)

Dead priests of Osiris and Isis,
  And Apis! that mystical lore,
Like a nightmare, conceived in a crisis
  Of fever, is studied no more;
Dead Magian! yon star-troop that spangles
  The arch of yon firmament vast
Looks calm, like a host of white angels,
  On dry dust of votaries past.

On seas unexplored can the ship shun
  Sunk rocks? Can man fathom life's links,
Past or future, unsolved by Egyptian
  Or Theban, unspoken by Sphinx?
The riddle remains still unravell'd
  By students consuming night oil.
Oh, earth! we have toil'd, we have travail'd,
  How long shall we travail and toil?

How long? The short life that fools reckon
  So sweet, by how much is it higher
Than brute life? — the false gods still beckon,
  And man, through the dust and the mire,
Toils onward, as toils the dull bullock,
  Unreasoning, brutish, and blind,
With Ashtaroth, Mammon, and Moloch
  In front, and Alecto behind.

The wise one of earth, the Chaldean,
  Serves folly in wisdom's disguise;
And the sensual Epicurean,
  Though grosser, is hardly less wise;
'Twixt the former, half pedant, half pagan,
  And the latter, half sow and half sloth,
We halt, choose Astarte or Dagon,

Or sacrifice freely to both.

With our reason that seeks to disparage,
 Brute instinct it fails to subdue;
With our false illegitimate courage,
 Our sophistry, vain and untrue;
Our hopes that ascend so and fall so,
 Our passions, fierce hates and hot loves,
We are wise (aye, the snake is wise also) —
 Wise as serpents, NOT harmless as doves.

Some flashes, like faint sparks from heaven,
 Come rarely with rushing of wings;
We are conscious at times we have striven,
 Though seldom, to grasp better things;
These pass, leaving hearts that have falter'd,
 Good angels with faces estranged,
And the skin of the Ethiop unalter'd,
 And the spots of the leopard unchanged.

Oh, earth! pleasant earth! have we hanker'd
 To gather thy flowers and thy fruits?
The roses are wither'd, and canker'd
 The lilies, and barren the roots
Of the fig-tree, the vine, the wild olive,
 Sharp thorns and sad thistles that yield
Fierce harvest — so WE live, and SO live
 The perishing beasts of the field.

And withal we are conscious of evil
 And good — of the spirit and the clod,
Of the power in our hearts of a devil,
 Of the power in our souls of a God,
Whose commandments are graven in no cypher,
 But clear as His sun — from our youth
One at least we have cherished — "An eye for
 An eye, and a tooth for a tooth."

Oh, man! of thy Maker the image;
 To passion, to pride, or to wealth,
Sworn bondsman, from dull youth to dim age,
 Thy portion the fire or the filth,
Dross seeking, dead pleasure's death rattle

Thy memories' happiest song,
And thy highest hope — scarce a drawn battle
With dark desperation. How long?

* * * * *

Roar louder! leap higher! ye surf-beds,
 And sprinkle your foam on the furze;
Bring the dreams that brought sleep to our turf-beds,
 To camps of our long ago years,
With the flashing and sparkling of broadswords,
 With the tossing of banners and spears,
With the trampling of hard hoofs on hard swards,
 With the mingling of trumpets and cheers.

* * * * *

The gale has gone down; yet outlasting
 The gale, raging waves of the sea,
Casting up their own foam, ever casting
 Their leprosy up with wild glee,
Still storm; so in rashness and rudeness
 Man storms through the days of his grace;
Yet man cannot fathom God's goodness,
 Exceeding God's infinite space.

And coldly and calmly and purely
 Grey rock and green hillock lie white
In star-shine dream-laden — so surely
 Night cometh — so cometh the night
When we, too, at peace with our neighbour,
 May sleep where God's hillocks are piled,
Thanking HIM for a rest from day's labour,
 And a sleep like the sleep of a child!

SCENE — The Castle in Normandy.

THORA working at embroidery, ELSPETH spinning.

Thora (sings):
We severed in autumn early,

Ere the earth was torn by the plough;
The wheat and the oats and the barley
 Are ripe for the harvest now.
We sunder'd one misty morning,
 Ere the hills were dimm'd by the rain,
Through the flowers those hills adorning —
 Thou comest not back again.

My heart is heavy and weary
 With the weight of a weary soul;
The mid-day glare grows dreary,
 And dreary the midnight scroll.
The corn-stalks sigh for the sickle,
 'Neath the load of the golden grain;
I sigh for a mate more fickle —
 Thou comest not back again.

The warm sun riseth and setteth,
 The night bringeth moistening dew,
But the soul that longeth forgetteth
 The warmth and the moisture too;
In the hot sun rising and setting
 There is naught save feverish pain;
There are tears in the night-dews wetting —
 Thou comest not back again.

Thy voice in mine ear still mingles
 With the voices of whisp'ring trees;
Thy kiss on my cheek still tingles
 At each kiss of the summer breeze;
While dreams of the past are thronging
 For substance of shades in vain,
I am waiting, watching, and longing —
 Thou comest not back again.

Waiting and watching ever,
 Longing and lingering yet,
Leaves rustle and corn-stalks quiver,
 Winds murmur and waters fret;
No answer they bring, no greeting,
 No speech save that sad refrain,
Nor voice, save an echo repeating —
 He cometh not back again.

Elspeth:
Thine eldest sister is wedded to Max;
　With Biorn, Hilda hath cast her lot.
If the husbands vanish'd, and left no tracks,
　Would the wives have cause for sorrow, I wot?

Thora:
How well I remember that dreary ride;
　How I sigh'd for the lands of ice and snow,
In the trackless wastes of the desert wide,
　With the sun o'erhead and the sand below;
'Neath the scanty shades of the feathery palms,
　How I sigh'd for the forest of sheltering firs,
Whose shadows environ'd the Danish farms,
　Where I sang and sported in childish years.
On the fourteenth day of our pilgrimage
　We stayed at the foot of a sandhill high;
Our fever'd thirst we could scarce assuage
　At the brackish well that was nearly dry,

And the hot sun rose, and the hot sun set,
　And we rode all the day through a desert land,
And we camp'd where the lake and the river met,
　On sedge and shingle and shining sand:
Enfolded in Hugo's cloak I slept,
　Or watch'd the stars while I lay awake;
And close to our feet the staghound crept,
　And the horses were grazing beside the lake;
Now we own castles and serving men,
　Lands and revenues. What of that?
Hugo the Norman was kinder then,
　And happier was Thora of Armorat.

Elspeth:
Nay, I warn'd thee, with Norman sails unfurl'd
　Above our heads, when we wished thee joy,
That men are the same all over the world,
　They will worship only the newest toy;
Yet Hugo is kind and constant too,
　Though somewhat given to studies of late;
Biorn is sottish, and Max untrue,
　And worse than thine is thy sisters' fate.
But a shadow darkens the chamber door.

Enter THURSTON.

Thurston:
'Tis I, Lady Thora; our lord is near.
My horse being fresher, I rode before;
Both he and Eric will soon be here.

Thora:
Good Thurston, give me your hand. You are
Most welcome. What has delayed you thus?

Thurston:
Both by sea and land we have travell'd far,
  Yet little of note has happened to us —
We were wreck'd on the shores of Brittany,
  Near the coast of Morbihan iron-bound;
The rocks were steep and the surf ran high,
  Thy kinsman, Eric, was well-nigh drown'd.
By a swarm of knaves we were next beset,
  Who took us for corsairs; then released
By a Breton count, whose name I forget.
  Now I go, by your leave, to tend my beast.
          [He goes out.]

Elspeth:
That man is rude and froward of speech:
  My ears are good, though my sight grows dim.

Thora:
Thurston is faithful. Thou canst not teach
  Courtly nor servile manners to him.

SCENE — The Castle Hall.

THURSTON, RALPH, EUSTACE, and other followers of HUGO, seated at a long table. HAROLD seated apart.

Thurston:
Who is that stranger, dark and tall,
On the wooden settle next to the wall —
Mountebank, pilgrim, or wandering bard?

Eustace:
To define his calling is somewhat hard;
Lady Thora has taken him by the hand
Because he has come from the Holy Land.
Pilgrims and palmers are all the rage
With her, since she shared in that pilgrimage
With Hugo. The stranger came yesterday,
And would have gone on, but she bade him stay.
Besides, he sings in the Danish tongue
The songs she has heard in her childhood sung.
That's all I know of him, good or bad;
In my own opinion he's somewhat mad.
You must raise your voice if you speak with him,
And he answers as though his senses were dim.

Thurston (to Harold):
Good-morrow, sir stranger.

Harold: Good-morrow, friend.

Thurston:
Where do you come from? and whither wend?

Harold:
I have travelled of late with the setting sun
At my back; and as soon as my task is done
I purpose to turn my face to the north —
Yet we know not what a day may bring forth.

Thurston:
Indeed we don't.

(To Eustace, aside):   Nay, I know him now
By that ugly scar that crosses his brow;
And the less we say to him the better.
Your judgment is right to the very letter —
The man is mad.

Eustace: But harmless, I think;
He eats but little, eschews strong drink,
And only speaks when spoken to first.

Thurston:
Harmless or not, he was once the worst
And bitterest foe Lord Hugo had;
And yet his story is somewhat sad.

Eustace:
May I hear it?

Thurston: Nay, I never reveal
What concerns me not. Our lord may conceal
Or divulge at pleasure his own affairs, —
Not even his comrade Eric shares
His secrets; though Eric thinks him wise,
Which is more than I do, for I despise
That foolish science he learnt in Rome.
He dreams and mopes when he sits at home,
And now he's not much better abroad;
'Tis hard to follow so tame a lord.
'Twixt us two, he won't be worth a rush
If he will persist in his studies — —

Eustace: Hush!
Ralph has persuaded our guest to sing.

Thurston:
I have known the day when his voice would ring
Till the rafters echoed.

Eustace: 'Tis pleasant still,
Though far too feeble this hall to fill.

Harold (sings):
On the current, where the wide
   Windings of the river
Eddy to the North Sea tide,
Shall I in my shallop glide,
As I have done at her side?
   Never! never! never!

In the forest, where the firs,
   Pines, and larches quiver
To the northern breeze that stirs,
Shall my lips be press'd to hers,

As they were in by-gone years?
   Never! never! never!

In the battle on the plain,
   Where the lance-shafts shiver,
And the sword-strokes fall like rain,
Shall I bear her scarf again
As I have done — not in vain?
   Never! never! never!

In a fairer, brighter land,
   Where the saints rest ever,
Shall I once more see her stand,
White, amidst a white-robed band,
Harp and palm-branch in her hand?
   Never! never! never!

SCENE — The Same.

EUSTACE, THURSTON, and followers of HUGO. HAROLD.

   Enter, by the hall door, HUGO, ERIC, and THORA.

Eustace (and others standing up):
Welcome, Lord Hugo!

Hugo: Welcome or not,
 Thanks for your greeting all.
Ha, Eustace! what complaints hast thou got?
 What grievances to recall?

Eustace:
Count William came with a numerous band,
 Ere the snows began to fall,
And slew a buck on your lordship's land,
 Within a league of the wall.

Hugo:
Count William has done to us no more
 Than we to him. In his vineyard
Last summer, or later, maybe, a boar

Was slaughter'd by Thurston's whinyard.

Thurston:
Aye, Hugo! But William kept the buck,
 I will wager marks a score,
Though the tale is new to me; and, worse luck,
 You made me give back the boar.

Harold (advancing):
Lord Hugo!

Hugo: What! Art thou living yet?
I scarcely knew thee, Sir Dane!
And 'tis not so very long since we met.

Harold:
'Twill be long ere we meet again. (gives a letter)
This letter was traced by one now dead
In the Holy Land; and I
Must wait till his dying request is read,
 And in his name ask the reply.

Thora (aside):
Who is that stranger, Hugo?

Hugo: By birth
He is a countryman of thine,
Thora. What writing is this on earth?
I can scarce decipher a line.

Harold:
The pen in the clutch of death works ill.

Hugo:
Nay, I read now; the letters run
More clearly.

Harold: Wilt grant the request?

Hugo: I will.

Harold:
Enough! Then my task is done. (He holds out his hand.)

Hugo, I go to a far-off land,
 Wilt thou say, "God speed thee!" now?
Hugo:
Sir Harold, I cannot take thy hand,
 Because of my ancient vow.

Harold:
Farewell, then.

Thora: Friend, till the morning wait.
 On so wild a night as this
Thou shalt not go from my husband's gate;
 The path thou wilt surely miss.

Harold:
I go. Kind lady, some future day
 Thy care will requited be.

Thora:
Speak, Hugo, speak.

Hugo: He may go or stay,
 It matters little to me.
         [Harold goes out.]

Thora:
Husband, that man is ill and weak;
 On foot he goes and alone
Through a barren moor in a night-storm bleak.

Eric:
Now I wonder where he has gone!

Hugo:
Indeed, I have not the least idea;
 The man is certainly mad.
He wedded my sister, Dorothea,
 And used her cruelly bad.
He was once my firmest and surest friend,
 And once my deadliest foe;
But hate and friendship both find their end —
 Now I heed not where he may go.

SCENE — A Chamber in the Castle.

HUGO, THORA, and ERIC.

Hugo:
That letter that came from Palestine,
 By the hands of yon wandering Dane,
Will cost me a pilgrimage to the Rhine.

Thora:
 Wilt thou travel so soon again?

Hugo:
I can scarce refuse the dying request
 Of my comrade, Baldwin, now;
His bones are dust. May his soul find rest
 He once made a foolish vow,
That at Englemehr, 'neath the watchful care
 Of the Abbess, his child should stay,
For a season at least. To escort her there
 I must start at the break of day.

Thora:
Is it Agatha that goes, or Clare?

Hugo:
 Nay, Clare is dwelling in Spain
With her spouse.

Thora: 'Tis Agatha. She is fair,
 I am told; but giddy and vain.

Eric:
Some musty tales on my memory grow
 Concerning Count Baldwin's vow;
Thou knew'st his daughter?

Hugo: Aye, years ago.
 I should scarcely know her now.
It seems, when her father's vow was made,
 She was taken sorely ill;
Then he travell'd, and on his return was stay'd;

He could never his oath fulfil.

Eric:
If rightly I've heard, 'twas Agatha
 That fled with some Danish knight —
I forget the name.

Hugo: Nay, she fled not far;
 She returned again that night.

Thora:
For a nun, I fear, she is too self-willed.

Hugo:
 That is no affair of mine.
My task is over, my word fulfilled,
 Should I bring her safe to the Rhine.
Come, Thora, sing.

Thora: Nay, I cannot sing,
 Nor would I now if I could.
Sing thou.

Hugo: I will, though my voice should bring
 No sound save a discord rude.
(Sings.)
Where the storm in its wrath hath lighted,
 The pine lies low in the dust;
And the corn is withered and blighted,
 Where the fields are red with the rust;
Falls the black frost, nipping and killing,
 Where its petals the violet rears,
And the wind, though tempered, is chilling
 To the lamb despoiled by the shears.

The strong in their strength are shaken,
 The wise in their wisdom fall;
And the bloom of beauty is taken —
 Strength, wisdom, beauty, and all,
They vanish, their lot fulfilling,
 Their doom approaches and nears,
But the wind, though tempered, is chilling
 To the lamb despoiled by the shears.

'Tis the will of a Great Creator,
  He is wise, His will must be done,
And it cometh sooner or later;
  And one shall be taken, and one
Shall be left here, toiling and tilling,
  In this vale of sorrows and tears,
Where the wind, though tempered, is chilling
  To the lamb despoiled by the shears.

Tell me, mine own one, tell me,
  The shadows of life and the fears
Shall neither daunt me nor quell me,
  While I can avert thy tears:
Dost thou shrink, as I shrink, unwilling
  To realise lonely years?
Since the wind, though tempered, is chilling
  To the lamb despoiled by the shears.

   Enter HENRY.

Henry:
My lord, Father Luke craves audience straight,
  He has come on foot from the chapel;
Some stranger perished beside his gate
  When the dawn began to dapple.

SCENE — A Chapel Not Very Far from Hugo's Castle.

HUGO, ERIC, and two Monks (LUKE and HUBERT). The dead body of HAROLD.

Luke:
  When the dawn was breaking,
    Came a faint sound, waking
Hubert and myself; we hurried to the door,
    Found the stranger lying
    At the threshold, dying.
Somewhere have I seen a face like his before.

Hugo:
  Harold he is hight.

Only yester-night
From our gates he wander'd, in the driving hail;
  Well his face I know,
  Both as friend and foe;
Of my followers only Thurston knows his tale.

Luke:
  Few the words he said,
  Faint the signs he made,
Twice or thrice he groaned; quoth Hubert, "Thou hast sinn'd.
  This is retribution,
  Seek for absolution;
Answer me — then cast thy sorrows to the wind.
  Do their voices reach thee,
  Friends who failed to teach thee,
In thine earlier days, to sunder right from wrong?
  Charges 'gainst thee cited,
  Cares all unrequited,
Counsels spurned and slighted — do they press and throng?"
  But he shook his head.
  "'Tis not so," he said;
"They will scarce reproach me who reproached of yore.
  If their counsels good,
  Rashly I withstood;
Having suffered longer, I have suffered more."

  "Do their curses stun thee?
  Foes who failed to shun thee,
Stricken by rash vengeance, in some wild career,
  As the barbed arrow
  Cleaveth bone and marrow,
From those chambers narrow — do they pierce thine ear?"
  And he made reply,
  Laughing bitterly,
"Did I fear them living — shall I fear them dead?
  Blood that I have spilt
  Leaveth little guilt;
On the hand it resteth, scarcely on the head."

  "Is there one whom thou
  May'st have wronged ere now,
Since remorse so sorely weigheth down thine heart?
  By some saint in heaven,

Sanctified and shriven,
Would'st thou be forgiven ere thy soul depart?"
　　Not a word he said,
　　But he bowed his head
Till his temples rested on the chilly sods
　　And we heard him groan —
　　"Ah! mine own, mine own!
If I had thy pardon I might ask for God's."

　　Hubert raised him slowly,
　　Sunrise, faint and holy,
Lit the dead face, placid as a child's might be.
　　May the troubled spirit,
　　Through Christ's saving merit,
Peace and rest inherit. Thus we sent for thee.

Hugo:
　　God o'erruleth fate.
　　I had cause for hate;
In this very chapel, years back, proud and strong,
　　Joined by priestly vows,
　　He became the spouse
Of my youngest sister, to her bitter wrong.
　　And he wrought her woe,
　　Making me his foe;
Not alone unfaithful — brutal, too, was he.
　　She had scarce been dead
　　Three months, ere he fled
With Count Baldwin's daughter, then betrothed to me.
　　Fortune straight forsook him,
　　Vengeance overtook him;
Heavy crimes will bring down heavy punishment.
　　All his strength was shatter'd,
　　Even his wits were scatter'd,
Half-deranged, half-crippled, wandering he went.
　　We are unforgiving
　　While our foes are living;
Yet his retribution weigh'd so heavily
　　That I feel remorse,
　　Gazing on his corpse,
For my rudeness when he left our gates to die.
　　And his grave shall be
　　'Neath the chestnut tree,

Where he met my sister many years ago;
   Leave that tress of hair
   On his bosom there —
Wrap the cerecloth round him! Eric, let us go.

SCENE — A Room in the Castle.

HUGO and ERIC. Early morning.

Hugo:
The morn is fair, the weary miles
Will shorten 'neath the summer's wiles;
Pomona in the orchard smiles,
 And in the meadow, Flora!
And I have roused a chosen band
For escort through the troubled land;
And shaken Elspeth by the hand,
 And said farewell to Thora.
Comrade and kinsman — for thou art
Comrade and kin to me — we part
Ere nightfall, if at once we start,
 We gain the dead Count's castle.
The roads are fair, the days are fine,
Ere long I hope to reach the Rhine.
Forsooth, no friend to me or mine
 Is that same Abbot Basil;
I thought he wronged us by his greed.
My father sign'd a foolish deed
For lack of gold in time of need,
 And thus our lands went by us;
Yet wrong on our side may have been:
As far as my will goes, I ween,
'Tis past, the grudge that lay between
 Us twain. Men call him pious —
And I have prosper'd much since then,
And gain'd for one lost acre ten;
And even the ancient house and glen
 Rebought with purchase-money.
He, too, is wealthy; he has got
By churchly rights a fertile spot,
A land of corn and wine, I wot,

A land of milk and honey.
Now, Eric, change thy plans and ride
With us; thou hast no ties, no bride.

Eric:
Nay, ties I have, and time and tide,
　Thou knowest, wait for no man;
And I go north; God's blessing shuns
The dwellings of forgetful sons,
That proverb he may read who runs,
　In Christian lore or Roman.
My good old mother she hath heard,
For twelve long months, from me no word;
At thought of her my heart is stirr'd,
　And even mine eyes grow moister.
Greet Ursula from me; her fame
Is known to all. A nobler dame,
Since days of Clovis, ne'er became
　The inmate of a cloister.
Our paths diverge, yet we may go
Together for a league or so;
I, too, will join thy band below
　When thou thy bugle windest.
　　　　[Eric goes out.]

Hugo:
From weaknesses we stand afar,
On us unpleasantly they jar;
And yet the stoutest-hearted are
　The gentlest and the kindest.
My mother loved me tenderly;
Alas! her only son was I.
I shudder'd, but my lids were dry,
　By death made orphan newly.
A braver man than me, I swear,
Who never comprehended fear,
Scarce names his mother, and the tear,
　Unbidden, springs unruly.

SCENE — A Road on the Norman Frontiers.

HUGO, AGATHA, ORION, THURSTON, and armed attendants, riding slowly.

Agatha:
Sir Knight, what makes you so grave and glum?
At times I fear you are deaf or dumb,
Or both.

Hugo: And yet, should I speak the truth,
There is little in common 'twixt us, forsooth;
You would think me duller, and still more vain,
If I uttered the thoughts that fill my brain;
Since the matters with which my mind is laden
Would scarcely serve to amuse a maiden.

Agatha:
I am so foolish and you are so wise,
'Tis the meaning your words so ill disguise.
Alas! my prospects are sad enough:
I had rather listen to speeches rough
Than muse and meditate silently
On the coming loss of my liberty.
Sad hope to me can my future bring,
Yet, while I may, I would prattle and sing,
Though it only were to try and assuage
The dreariness of my pilgrimage.

Hugo:
Prattle and sing to your heart's content,
And none will offer impediment.

Agatha (sings):
We were playmates in childhood, my sister and I,
 Whose playtime with childhood is done;
Through thickets where briar and bramble grew high,
 Barefooted I've oft seen her run.

I've known her, when mists on the moorland hung white,
 Bareheaded past nightfall remain;
She has followed a landless and penniless knight

Through battles and sieges in Spain.

But I pulled the flower, and shrank from the thorn,
 Sought the sunshine, and fled from the mist;
My sister was born to face hardship with scorn —
 I was born to be fondled and kiss'd.

Hugo (aside):
She has a sweet voice.

Orion: And a sweet face, too —
Be candid for once, and give her her due.

Agatha:
Your face grows longer, and still more long,
Sir Scholar! how did you like my song?

Hugo:
I thought it rather a silly one.

Agatha:
You are far from a pleasant companion.

SCENE — An Apartment in a Wayside Inn.

HUGO and AGATHA. Evening.

Hugo:
I will leave you now — we have talked enough,
 And for one so tenderly reared and nursed
This journey is wearisome, perhaps, and rough.

Agatha: Will you not finish your story first?

Hugo:
I repent me that I began it now,
 'Tis a dismal tale for a maiden's ears;
Your cheek is pale already, your brow
 Is sad, and your eyes are moist with tears.

Agatha:
It may be thus, I am lightly vexed,
  But the tears will lightly come and go;
I can cry one moment and laugh the next,
  Yet I have seen terrors, as well you know.
I remember that flight through moss and fern,
  The moonlit shadows, the hoofs that rolled
In fierce pursuit, and the ending stern,
  And the hawk that left his prey on the wold.

Hugo:
I have sorrowed since that I left you there:
  Your friends were close behind on the heath,
Though not so close as I thought they were.
(Aside.) Now I will not tell her of Harold's death.

Agatha:
'Tis true, I was justly punished, and men,
  As a rule, of pity have little share;
Had I died you had cared but little then.

Hugo: But little then, yet now I should care
More than you think for. Now, good-night.
  Tears still? Ere I leave you, child, alone,
Must I dry your cheeks?

Agatha: Nay, I am not quite
Such a child but what I can dry my own.
          [Hugo goes out. Agatha retires.]

Orion (singing outside the window of Agatha's chamber):

'Neath the stems with blossoms laden,
  'Neath the tendrils curling,
I, thy servant, sing, oh, maiden!
  I, thy slave, oh, darling!
Lo! the shaft that slew the red deer,
  At the elk may fly too.
Spare them not! The dead are dead, dear,
  Let the living die too.

Where the wiles of serpent mingle,
  And the looks of dove lie,

Where small hands in strong hands tingle,
  Loving eyes meet lovely:
Where the harder natures soften,
  And the softer harden —
Certes! such things have been often
  Since we left Eve's garden.

Sweeter follies herald sadder
  Sins — look not too closely;
Tongue of asp and tooth of adder
  Under leaf of rose lie.
Warned, advised in vain, abandon
  Warning and advice too,
Let the child lay wilful hand on
  Den of cockatrice too.

I, thy servant, or thy master,
  One or both — no matter;
If the former — firmer, faster,
  Surer still the latter —
Lull thee, soothe thee with my singing,
  Bid thee sleep, and ponder
On my lullabies still ringing
  Through thy dreamland yonder.

SCENE — A Wooded Rising Ground, Near the Rhine.

HUGO and AGATHA resting under the trees. THURSTON, EUSTACE, and followers a little apart. ORION. (Noonday.) The Towers of the Convent in the distance.

Agatha:
I sit on the greensward, and hear the bird sing,
'Mid the thickets where scarlet and white blossoms cling;
And beyond the sweet uplands all golden with flower,
It looms in the distance, the grey convent tower.
And the emerald earth and the sapphire-hued sky
Keep telling me ever my spring has gone by;
Ah! spring premature, they are tolling thy knell,
In the wind's soft adieu, in the bird's sweet farewell.
Oh! why is the greensward with garlands so gay,

That I quail at the sight of my prison-house grey?
Oh! why is the bird's note so joyous and clear?
The caged bird must pine in a cage doubly drear.

Hugo:
May the lances of Dagobert harry their house,
If they coax or intimidate thee to take vows;
May the freebooters pillage their shrines, should they dare
Touch with their scissors thy glittering hair.
Our short and sweet journey now draws to an end,
And homeward my sorrowful way I must wend;
Oh, fair one! oh, loved one! I would I were free,
To squander my life in the greenwood with thee.

Orion (aside):
Ho! seeker of knowledge, so grave and so wise,
Touch her soft curl again — look again in her eyes;
Forget for the nonce musty parchments, and learn
How the slow pulse may quicken — the cold blood may burn.
Ho! fair, fickle maiden, so blooming and shy!
The old love is dead, let the old promise die!
Thou dost well, thou dost wise, take the word of Orion,
"A living dog always before a dead lion!"

* * * * *

Thurston:
Ye varlets, I would I knew which of ye burst
Our wine-skin — what, ho! must I perish with thirst!
Go, Henry, thou hast a glib tongue, go and ask
Thy lord to send Ralph to yon inn for a flask.

Henry:
Nay, Thurston, not so; I decline to disturb
Our lord for the present; go thou, or else curb
Thy thirst, or drink water, as I do.

Thurston: Thou knave
Of a page, dost thou wish me the colic to have?

Orion (aside):
That clown is a thoroughbred Saxon. He thinks
With pleasure on naught save hard blows and strong drinks;

In hell he will scarce go athirst if once given
An inkling of any good liquors in heaven.

* * * * *

Hugo:
Our Pontiff to manhood at Englemehr grew,
The priests there are many, the nuns are but few.
I love not the Abbot — 'tis needless to tell
My reason; but all of the Abbess speak well.

Agatha:
Through vineyards and cornfields beneath us, the Rhine
Spreads and winds, silver-white, in the merry sunshine;
And the air, overcharged with a subtle perfume,
Grows faint from the essence of manifold bloom.

Hugo:
And the tinkling of bells, and the bleating of sheep,
And the chaunt from the fields, where the labourers reap
The earlier harvest, comes faint on the breeze,
That whispers so faintly in hedgerows and trees.

Orion:
And a waggon wends slow to those turrets and spires,
To feed the fat monks and the corpulent friars;
It carries the corn, and the oil, and the wine,
The honey and milk from the shores of the Rhine.
The oxen are weary and spent with their load,
They pause, but the driver doth recklessly goad;
Up yon steep, flinty rise they have staggered and reeled,
Even devils may pity dumb beasts of the field.

Agatha (sings):

Oh! days and years departed,
Vain hopes, vain fears that smarted,
I turn to you sad-hearted —
   I turn to you in tears!
Your daily sun shone brightly,
Your happy dreams came nightly,
Flowers bloomed and birds sang lightly,
   Through all your hopes and fears!

You halted not, nor tarried,
Your hopes have all miscarried,
And even your fears are buried,
   Since fear with hope must die.
You halted not, but hasted,
And flew past, childhood wasted,
And girlhood scarcely tasted,
   Now womanhood is nigh.

Yet I forgive your wronging,
Dead seasons round me thronging,
With yearning and with longing,
   I call your bitters sweet.
Vain longing, and vain yearning,
There now is no returning;
Oh! beating heart and burning,
   Forget to burn and beat!

Oh! childish suns and showers,
Oh! girlish thorns and flowers,
Oh! fruitless days and hours,
   Oh! groundless hopes and fears:
The birds still chirp and twitter,
And still the sunbeams glitter:
Oh! barren years and bitter,
   Oh! bitter, barren years!

SCENE — The Summit of a Burning Mountain.

Night. A terrific storm. ORION (undisguised).

Orion (sings):
From fathomless depths of abysses,
 Where fires unquenchable burst,
From the blackness of darkness, where hisses
 The brood of the serpent accurs'd;
From shrines where the hymns are the weeping
 And wailing and gnashing of teeth,
Where the palm is the pang never sleeping,
 Where the worm never dying is the wreath;
Where all fruits save wickedness wither,

Whence naught save despair can be gleaned —
Come hither! come hither! come hither!
Fall'n angel, fell sprite, and foul fiend.
Come hither! the bands are all broken,
  And loosed in hell's innermost womb,
When the spell unpronounceable spoken
  Divides the unspeakable gloom.

    Evil Spirits approach. The storm increases.

Evil Spirits (singing):
We hear thee, we seek thee, on pinions
  That darken the shades of the shade;
Oh! Prince of the Air, with dominions
  Encompass'd, with powers array'd,
With majesty cloth'd as a garment,
  Begirt with a shadowy shine,
Whose feet scorch the hill-tops that are meant
  As footstools for thee and for thine.

Orion (sings):
How it swells through each pause of the thunder,
  And mounts through each lull of the gust,
Through the crashing of crags torn asunder,
  And the hurtling of trees in the dust;
With a chorus of loud lamentations,
  With its dreary and hopeless refrain!
'Tis the cry of all tongues and all nations,
  That suffer and shudder in vain.

Evil Spirits (singing):
'Tis the cry of all tongues and all nations;
  Our song shall chime in with their strain;
Lost spirits blend their wild exultations
  With the sighing of mortals in pain.

Orion (sings):
With just light enough to see sorrows
  In this world, and terrors beyond,
'Twixt the day's bitter pangs and the morrow's
  Dread doubts, to despair and despond,
Man lingers through toils unavailing
  For blessings that baffle his grasp;

To his cradle he comes with a wailing,
 He goes to his grave with a gasp.

Evil Spirits (singing):
His birth is a weeping and wailing,
 His death is a groan and a gasp;
O'er the seed of the woman prevailing,
 Thus triumphs the seed of the asp.

SCENE — Chamber of a Wayside Inn.

HUGO sitting alone. Evening.

Hugo:
And now the parting is over,
 The parting should end the pain;
And the restless heart may recover,
 And so may the troubled brain.
I am sitting within the chamber
 Whose windows look on the porch,
Where the roses cluster and clamber;
 We halted here on our march
With her to the convent going,
 And now I go back alone:
Ye roses, budding and blowing,
 Ye heed not though she is flown.

I remember the girlish gesture,
 The sportive and childlike grace,
With which she crumpled and pressed your
 Rose leaves to her rose-hued face.
Shall I think on her ways hereafter —
 On those flashes of mirth and grief,
On that April of tears and laughter,
 On our parting, bitterly brief?

I remember the bell at sunrise,
 That sounded so solemnly,
Bidding monk, and prelate, and nun rise;
 I rose ere the sun was high.
Down the long, dark, dismal passage,

To the door of her resting-place
I went, on a farewell message,
I trod with a stealthy pace.
There was no one there to see us
 When she opened her chamber door.
"Miserere, mei Deus",
 Rang faint from the convent choir.

I remember the dark and narrow
 And scantily-furnished room;
And the gleam, like a golden arrow —
 The gleam that lighted the gloom.
One couch, one seat, and one table,
 One window, and only one —
It stands in the eastern gable,
 It faces the rising sun;
One ray shot through it, and one light
 On doorway and threshold played.
She stood within in the sunlight,
 I stood without in the shade.

I remember that bright form under
 The sheen of that slanting ray.
I spoke — "For life we must sunder,
 Let us sunder without delay.
Let us sever without preamble,
 As brother and sister part,
For the sake of one pleasant ramble,
 That will live in at least one heart."
Still the choir in my ears rang faintly,
 In the distance dying away,
Sweetly and sadly and saintly,
 Through arch and corridor grey!

And thus we parted for ever,
 Between the shade and the shine;
Not as brother and sister sever —
 I fondled her hands in mine.
Still the choir in my ears rang deaden'd
 And dull'd, though audible yet;
And she redden'd, and paled, and redden'd —
 Her lashes and lids grew wet.
Not as brother severs from sister,

My lips clung fast to her lips;
She shivered and shrank when I kissed her.
On the sunbeam drooped the eclipse.

I remember little of the parting
 With the Abbot, down by the gate,
My men were eager for starting;
 I think he pressed me to wait.
From the lands where convent and glebe lie,
 From manors, and Church's right,
Where I fought temptation so feebly,
 I, too, felt eager for flight.
Alas! the parting is over —
 The parting, but not the pain —
Oh! sweet was the purple clover,
 And sweet was the yellow grain;
And sweet were the woody hollows
 On the summery Rhineward track;
But a winter untimely swallows
 All sweets as I travel back.

Yet I feel assured, in some fashion,
 Ere the hedges are crisp with rime,
I shall conquer this senseless passion,
 'Twill yield to toil and to time.
I will fetter these fancies roaming;
 Already the sun has dipped;
I will trim the lamps in the gloaming,
 I will finish my manuscript.
Through the nightwatch unflagging study
 Shall banish regrets perforce;
As soon as the east is ruddy
 Our bugle shall sound "To Horse!"

SCENE — Another Wayside House, Near the Norman Frontier.

HUGO and ORION in a chamber. Evening.

Orion:
Your eyes are hollow, your step is slow,
 And your cheek is pallid as though from toil,

Watching or fasting, by which I know
 That you have been burning the midnight oil.

Hugo:
Aye, three nights running.

Orion: 'Twill never do
 To travel all day, and study all night;
Will you join in a gallop through mist and dew,
 In a flight that may vie with the eagle's flight?

Hugo:
With all my heart. Shall we saddle "Rollo"?

Orion:
 Nay, leave him undisturb'd in his stall;
I have steeds he would hardly care to follow.

Hugo:
 Follow, forsooth! he can lead them all.

Orion:
Touching his merits we will not quarrel;
 But let me mount you for once; enough
Of work may await your favourite sorrel,
 And the paths we must traverse to-night are rough.
But first let me mix you a beverage,
 To invigorate your enfeebled frame.
   [He mixes a draught and hands it to Hugo.]
All human ills this draught can assuage.

Hugo:
It hisses and glows like liquid flame;
Say, what quack nostrum is this thou'st brewed?
Speak out; I am learned in the chemist's lore.

Orion:
There is nothing but what will do you good;
 And the drugs are simples; 'tis hellebore,
Nepenthe, upas, and dragon's blood,
 Absinthe, and mandrake, and mandragore.

Hugo:
I will drink it, although, by mass and rood,
 I am just as wise as I was before.

SCENE — A Rough, Hilly Country.

HUGO and ORION riding at speed on black horses.
Mountains in the distance. Night.

Hugo:
See! the sparks that fly from our hoof-strokes make
A fiery track that gleams in our wake;
Like a dream the dim landscape past us shoots,
Our horses fly.

Orion: They are useful brutes,
Though somewhat skittish; the foam is whit'ning
The crest and rein of my courser "Lightning";
He pulls to-night, being short of work,
And takes his head with a sudden jerk;
Still heel and steady hand on the bit,
For that is "Tempest" on which you sit.

Hugo:
'Tis the bravest steed that ever I back'd;
Did'st mark how he crossed yon cataract?
From hoof to hoof I should like to measure
The space he clear'd.

Orion: He can clear at leisure
A greater distance. Observe the chasm
We are nearing. Ha! did you feel a spasm
As we flew over it?

Hugo: Not at all.

Orion:
Nathless 'twas an ugly place for a fall.

Hugo:
Let us try a race to yon mountain high,

That rears its dusky peak 'gainst the sky.
Orion:
I won't disparage your horsemanship,
But your steed will stand neither spur nor whip,
And is hasty and hard to steer at times.
We must travel far ere the midnight chimes;
We must travel back ere the east is grey.
Ho! "Lightning"! "Tempest"! Away! Away!
      [They ride on faster.]

SCENE — A Peak in a Mountainous Country Overhanging a Rocky Pass.

HUGO and ORION on black horses. Midnight.

Hugo:
These steeds are sprung from no common race,
Their vigour seems to annihilate space;
What hast thou brought me here to see?

Orion:
No boisterous scene of unhallow'd glee,
No sabbat of witches coarse and rude,
But a mystic and musical interlude;
You have long'd to explore the scrolls of Fate,
Dismount, as I do, and listen and wait.
      [They dismount.]

Orion (chanting):
Spirits of earth, and air, and sea,
 Spirits unclean, and spirits untrue,
By the symbols three that shall nameless be,
 One of your masters calls on you.

Spirits (chanting in the distance):
From the bowels of earth, where gleams the gold;
From the air where the powers of darkness hold
   Their court; from the white sea-foam,
Whence the white rose-tinted goddess sprung,
Whom poets of every age have sung,
   Ever we come! we come!

Hugo:
How close to our ears the thunder peals!
How the earth beneath us shudders and reels!

A Voice (chanting):
Woe to the earth! Where men give death!
    And women give birth!
To the sons of Adam, by Cain or Seth!
    Plenty and dearth!
To the daughters of Eve, who toil and spin,
    Barren of worth!
Let them sigh, and sicken, and suffer sin!
    Woe to the earth!

Hugo:
What is yon phantom large and dim
That over the mountain seems to swim?

Orion:
'Tis the scarlet woman of Babylon!

Hugo:
Whence does she come? Where has she gone?
And who is she?

Orion: You would know too much;
These are subjects on which I dare not touch;
And if I were to try and enlighten you,
I should probably fail, and possibly frighten you.
You had better ask some learned divine,
Whose opinion is p'rhaps worth as much as mine,
In his own conceit; and who, besides,
Could tell you the brand of the beast she rides.
What can you see in the valley yonder?
Speak out; I can hear you, for all the thunder.

Hugo:
I see four shadowy altars rise,
They seem to swell and dilate in size;
Larger and clearer now they loom,
Now fires are lighting them through the gloom.

A Voice (chanting):
The first a golden-hued fire shows,
A blood-red flame on the second glows,
The blaze on the third is tinged like the rose,
From the fourth a column of black smoke goes.

Orion:
Can you see all this?

Hugo: I see and hear;
The lights and hues are vivid and clear.

Spirits (sing at the first altar):
Hail, Mammon! while man buys and barters,
 Thy kingdom in this world is sure;
Thy prophets thou hast and thy martyrs,
 Great things in thy name they endure;
Thy fetters of gold crush the miser,
 The usurer bends at thy shrine,
And the wealthier nations and the wiser
 Bow with us at this altar of thine.

Spirits (sing at the second altar):
Hail, Moloch! whose banner floats blood-red,
 From pole to equator unfurl'd,
Whose laws redly written have stood red,
 And shall stand while standeth this world;
Clad in purple, with thy diadem gory,
 Thy sceptre the blood-dripping steel,
Thy subjects with us give thee glory,
 With us at thine altar they kneel.

Spirits (sing at the third altar):
Hail, Sovereign! whose fires are kindled
 By sparks from the bottomless pit,
Has thy worship diminish'd or dwindled?
 Do the yokes of thy slaves lightly sit?
Nay, the men of all climes and all races
 Are stirr'd by the flames that now stir us;
Then (as we do) they fall on their faces,
 Crying, "Hear us! Oh! Ashtaroth, hear us!"

Spirits (all in chorus):
The vulture her carrion swallows,
 Returns to his vomit the dog.
In the slough of uncleanliness wallows
 The he-goat, and revels the hog.
Men are wise with their schools and their teachers,
 Men are just with their creeds and their priests;
Yet, in spite of their pedants and preachers,
 They backslide in footprints of beasts!

Hugo:
From the smoky altar there seems to come
A stifled murmur, a droning hum.

Orion:
With that we have nothing at all to do,
Or, at least, not now, neither I nor you;
Though some day or other, possibly
We may see it closer, both you and I;
Let us visit the nearest altar first,
Whence the yellow fires flicker and burst,
Like the flames from molten ore that spring;
We may stand in the pale of the outer ring,
But forbear to trespass within the inner,
Lest the sins of the past should find out the sinner.
            [They approach the first altar, and stand within the
            outer circle which surrounds it, and near the inner.]

Spirits (sing):
Beneath us it flashes,
 The glittering gold,
Though it turneth to ashes
 And dross in the hold;
Yet man will endeavour,
 By fraud or by strife,
To grasp it and never
 To yield it with life.

Orion:
What can you see?

Hugo: Some decrepit shapes,
That are neither dwarfs, nor demons, nor apes;

In the hollow earth they appear to store
And rake together great heaps of ore.
Orion:
These are the gnomes, coarse sprites and rough;
Come on, of these we have seen enough.
   [They approach second altar and stand as before.]

Spirits (singing):
Above us it flashes,
 The glittering steel,
Though the red blood splashes
 Where its victims reel;
Yet man will endeavour
 To grapple the hilt,
And to wield the blade ever
 Till his life be spilt.

Orion:
What see you now?

Hugo: A rocky glen,
A horrid jumble of fighting men,
And a face that somewhere I've seen before.

Orion:
Come on; there is naught worth seeing more,
Except the altar of Ashtaroth.

Hugo:
To visit that altar I am loth.

Orion:
Why so?

Hugo: Nay, I cannot fathom why,
But I feel no curiosity.

Orion:
Come on. Stand close to the inner ring,
And hear how sweetly these spirits sing.
   [They approach third altar.]

Spirits (sing):
Around us it flashes,
 The cestus of one
Born of white foam, that dashes
 Beneath the white sun;
Let the mortal take heart, he
 Has nothing to dare;
She is fair, Queen Astarte,
 Her subjects are fair!

Orion:
What see you now, friend?

Hugo: Wood and wold,
And forms that look like the nymphs of old.
There is nothing here worth looking at twice.
I have seen enough.

Orion: You are far too nice;
Nevertheless, you must look again.
Those forms will fade.

Hugo: They are growing less plain.
They vanish. I see a door that seems
To open; a ray of sunlight gleams
From a window behind; a vision as fair
As the flush of dawn is standing there.
       [He gazes earnestly.]

Orion (sings):
Higher and hotter the white flames glow,
And the adamant may be thaw'd like snow,
And the life for a single chance may go,
 And the soul for a certainty.
Oh! vain and shallow philosopher,
Dost feel them quicken, dost feel them stir,
The thoughts that have stray'd again to HER
 From whom thou hast sought to fly?

Lo! the furnace is heated till sevenfold;
Is thy brain still calm? Is thy blood still cold
To the curls that wander in ripples of gold,
 On the shoulders of ivory?

Do the large, dark eyes, and the small, red mouth,
Consume thine heart with a fiery drouth,
Like the fierce sirocco that sweeps from the south,
   When the deserts are parch'd and dry?

Aye, start and shiver and catch thy breath,
The sting is certain, the venom is death,
And the scales are flashing the fruit beneath,
   And the fang striketh suddenly.
At the core the ashes are bitter and dead,
But the rind is fair and the rind is red,
It has ever been pluck'd since the serpent said,
   Thou shalt NOT SURELY die.

      [Hugo tries to enter the inner ring;
      Orion holds him back; they struggle.]

Hugo:
Unhand me, slave! or quail to the rod!
Agatha! Speak! in the name of God!

      [The vision disappears; the altars vanish.
      Hugo falls insensible.]

SCENE — The Wayside House.

HUGO waking in his chamber. ORION unseen at first. Morning.

Hugo:
Vanish, fair and fatal vision!
 Fleeting shade of fever'd sleep,
Chiding one whose indecision
 Waking substance failed to keep;
Picture into life half starting,
 As in life once seen before,
Parting somewhat sadly, parting
 Slowly at the chamber door.

Were my waking senses duller?
 Have I seen with mental eye
Light and shade, and warmth and colour,

Plainer than reality?
Sunlight that on tangled tresses
 Every ripple gilds and tips;
Balm and bloom, and breath of kisses,
 Warm on dewy, scarlet lips.

Dark eyes veiling half their splendour
 'Neath their lashes' darker fringe,
Dusky, dreamy, deep and tender,
 Passing smile and passing tinge;
Dimpling fast and flushing faster,
 Ivory chin and coral cheek,
Pearly strings, by alabaster
 Neck and arms made faint and weak;

Drooping, downcast lids enduring
 Gaze of man unwillingly;
Sudden, sidelong gleams alluring,
 Partly arch and partly shy.
Do I bless or curse that beauty?
 Am I longing, am I loth?
Is it passion, is it duty
 That I strive with, one or both?

Round about one fiery centre
 Wayward thoughts like moths revolve.
   [He sees Orion.]
Ha! Orion, thou didst enter
 Unperceived. I pray thee solve
These two questions: Firstly, tell me,
 Must I strive for wrong or right?
Secondly, what things befell me —
 Facts, or phantasies — last night?

Orion:
First, your strife is all a sham, you
 Know as well as I which wins;
Second, waking sins will damn you,
 Never mind your sleeping sins;
Both your questions thus I answer;
 Listen, ere you seek or shun:
I at least am no romancer,
 What you long for may be won.

Turn again and travel Rhineward,
  Tread once more the flowery path.

Hugo:
Aye, the flowery path that, sinward
  Pointing, ends in sin and wrath.

Orion:
Songs by love-birds lightly caroll'd,
  Even the just man may allure.

Hugo:
To his shame; in this wise Harold
  Sinn'd, his punishment was sure.

Orion:
Nay, the Dane was worse than you are,
  Base and pitiless to boot;
Doubtless all are bad, yet few are
  Cruel, false, and dissolute.

Hugo:
Some sins foreign to our nature
  Seem; we take no credit when
We escape them.

Orion: Yet the creature,
  Sin-created, lives to sin.

Hugo:
Be it so; come good, come evil,
  Ride we to the Rhine again!

Orion (aside):
'Gainst the logic of the devil
  Human logic strives in vain.

SCENE — A Camp Near the Black Forest.

RUDOLPH, OSRIC, DAGOBERT, and followers. ORION disguised as one of the Free-lances. Mid-day.

Osric:
Now, by axe of Odin, and hammer of Thor,
And by all the gods of the Viking's war,
I swear we have quitted our homes in vain:
We have nothing to look to, glory nor gain.
Will our galley return to Norway's shore
With heavier gold, or with costlier store?
Will our exploits furnish the scald with a song?
We have travell'd too far, we have tarried too long.
Say, captains all, is there ever a village
For miles around that is worth the pillage?
Will it pay the costs of my men or yours
To harry the homesteads of German boors?
Have we cause for pride in our feats of arms
When we plunder the peasants or sack the farms?
I tell thee, Rudolph of Rothenstein,
That were thy soldiers willing as mine,
And I sole leader of this array,
I would give Prince Otto battle this day.
Dost thou call thy followers men of war?
Oh, Dagobert! thou whose ancestor
On the neck of the Caesar's offspring trod,
Who was justly surnamed "The Scourge of God".
Yet in flight lies safety. Skirmish and run
To forest and fastness, Teuton and Hun,
From the banks of the Rhine to the Danube's shore,
And back to the banks of the Rhine once more;
Retreat from the face of an armed foe,
Robbing garden and hen-roost where'er you go.
Let the short alliance betwixt us cease,
I and my Norsemen will go in peace!
I wot it never will suit with us,
Such existence, tame and inglorious;
I could live no worse, living single-handed,
And better with half my men disbanded.

Rudolph:
Jarl Osric, what would'st thou have me do?
'Gainst Otto's army our men count few;
With one chance of victory, fight, say I!
But not when defeat is a certainty.
If Rudiger joins us with his free-lances,
Our chance will be equal to many chances;

For Rudiger is both prompt and wary;
And his men are gallant though mercenary;
But the knave refuses to send a lance
Till half the money is paid in advance.

Dagobert:
May his avarice wither him like a curse!
I guess he has heard of our late reverse;
But, Rudolph, whether he goes or stays,
There is reason in what Jarl Osric says;
Of provisions we need a fresh supply,
And our butts and flasks are shallow or dry;
My men are beginning to grumble sadly,
'Tis no wonder, since they must fare so badly.

Rudolph:
We have plenty of foragers out, and still
We have plenty of hungry mouths to fill;
And, moreover, by some means, foul or fair,
We must raise money; 'tis little I care,
So long as we raise it, whence it comes.

Osric:
Shall we sit till nightfall biting our thumbs?
The shortest plan is ever the best;
Has anyone here got aught to suggest?

Orion:
The cornfields are golden that skirt the Rhine,
Fat are the oxen, strong is the wine,
In those pleasant pastures, those cellars deep,
That o'erflow with the tears that those vineyards weep;
Is it silver you stand in need of, or gold?
Ingot or coin? There is wealth untold
In the ancient convent of Englemehr;
That is not so very far from here.
The Abbot, esteem'd a holy man,
Will hold what he has and grasp what he can;
The cream of the soil he loves to skim,
Why not levy a contribution on him?

Dagobert:
The stranger speaks well; not far away

That convent lies; and one summer's day
Will suffice for a horseman to reach the gate;
The garrison soon would capitulate,
Since the armed retainers are next to none,
And the walls, I wot, may be quickly won.

Rudolph:
I kept those walls for two months or more,
When they feared the riders of Melchior!
That was little over three years ago.
Their Abbot is thrifty, as well I know;
He haggled sorely about the price
Of our service.

Dagobert: Rudolph, he paid thee twice.

Rudolph:
Well, what of that? Since then I've tried
To borrow from him; now I know he lied
When he told me he could not spare the sum
I asked. If we to his gates should come,
He could spare it though it were doubled; and still,
This war with the Church I like it ill.

Osric:
The creed of our fathers is well-nigh dead,
And the creed of the Christian reigns in its stead
But the creed of the Christian, too, may die,
For your creeds or your churches what care I!
If there be plunder at Englemehr,
Let us strike our tents and thitherward steer.

SCENE — A Farm-house on the Rhine (About a mile from the Convent).

HUGO in chamber alone. Enter ERIC.

Eric:
What, Hugo, still at the Rhine! I thought
You were home. You have travell'd by stages short.

Hugo (with hesitation):
Our homeward march was labour in vain,
We had to retrace our steps again;
It was here or hereabouts that I lost
Some papers of value; at any cost
I must find them; and which way lies your course?

Eric:
I go to recruit Prince Otto's force.
I cannot study as you do; I
Am wearied with inactivity;
So I carry a blade engrim'd with rust
(That a hand sloth-slacken'd has, I trust,
Not quite forgotten the way to wield),
To strike once more on the tented field.

Hugo:
Fighting is all a mistake, friend Eric,
And has been so since the age Homeric,
When Greece was shaken and Troy undone,
Ten thousand lives for a worthless one.
Yet I blame you not; you might well do worse;
Better fight and perish than live to curse
The day you were born; and such has been
The lot of many, and shall, I ween,
Be the lot of more. If Thurston chooses
He may go with you. The blockhead abuses
Me and the life I lead.

    Enter ORION.

Orion: Great news!
The Englemehr monks will shake in their shoes;
In the soles of their callous feet will shake
The barefooted friars. The nuns will quake.

Hugo: Wherefore?

Orion: The outlaw of Rothenstein
Has come with his soldiers to the Rhine,
Back'd by those hardy adventurers
From the northern forests of pines and firs,
And Dagobert's horse. They march as straight

As the eagle swoops to the convent gate.

Hugo:
We must do something to save the place.

Orion:
They are sure to take it in any case,
Unless the sum that they ask is paid.

Eric:
Some effort on our part must be made.

Hugo:
'Tis not so much for the monks I care.

Eric:
Nor I; but the Abbess and nuns are there.

Orion:
'Tis not our business; what can we do?
They are too many, and we are too few;
And yet, I suppose, you will save, if you can,
That lady, your ward, or your kinswoman.

Hugo:
She is no kinswoman of mine;
How far is Otto's camp from the Rhine?

Orion:
Too far for help in such time of need
To be brought, though you used your utmost speed.

Eric:
Nay, that I doubt.

Hugo: And how many men
Have they?

Orion: To your one they could muster ten.

Eric:
I know Count Rudolph, and terms may be made
With him, I fancy; for though his trade

Is a rough one now, gainsay it who can,
He was once a knight and a gentleman.
And Dagobert, the chief of the Huns,
Bad as he is, will spare the nuns;
Though neither he nor the Count could check
Those lawless men, should they storm and sack
The convent. Jarl Osric, too, I know;
He is rather a formidable foe,
And will likely enough be troublesome;
But the others, I trust, to terms will come.

Hugo:
Eric, how many men have you?
I can count a score.

Eric: I have only two.

Hugo:
At every hazard we must try to save
The nuns.

Eric: Count Rudolph shall think we have
A force that almost equals his own,
If I can confer with him alone.

Orion:
He is close at hand; by this time he waits
The Abbot's reply at the convent gates.

Hugo:
We had better send him a herald.

Eric: Nay,
I will go myself.   [Eric goes out.]

Hugo: Orion, stay!
So this is the reed on which I've leaned,
 These are the hopes thou hast fostered, these
The flames thou hast fanned. Oh, lying fiend!
 Is it thus thou dost keep thy promises?

Orion:
Strong language, Hugo, and most unjust;

You will cry out before you are hurt —
You will live to recall your words, I trust.
 Fear nothing from Osric or Dagobert,
These are your friends, if you only knew it,
 And would take the advice of a friend sincere;
Neglect his counsels and you must rue it,
 For I know by a sign the crisis is near.
Accept the terms of these outlaws all,
 And be thankful that things have fallen out
Exactly as you would have had them fall —
 You may save the one that you care about;
Otherwise, how did you hope to gain
 Access to her — on what pretence?
What were the schemes that worried your brain
 To tempt her there or to lure her thence?
You must have bungled, and raised a scandal
 About your ears, that might well have shamed
The rudest Hun, the veriest Vandal,
 Long or ever the bird was tamed.

Hugo:
The convent is scarce surrounded yet,
 We might reach and hold it against their force
Till another sun has risen and set;
 And should I despatch my fleetest horse
To Otto — —

Orion: For Abbot, or Monk, or Friar,
 Between ourselves, 'tis little you care
If their halls are harried by steel and fire:
 Their avarice left your heritage bare.
Forsake them! Mitres, and cowls, and hoods
 Will cover vices while earth endures;
Through the green and gold of the summer woods
 Ride out with that pretty bird of yours.
If again you fail to improve your chance,
 Why, then, my friend, I can only say
You are duller far than the dullest lance
 That rides in Dagobert's troop this day.
"Faemina semper", frown not thus,
 The girl was always giddy and wild,
Vain, and foolish, and frivolous,
 Since she fled from her father's halls, a child.

I sought to initiate you once
 In the mystic lore of the old Chaldean;
But I found you far too stubborn a dunce,
 And your tastes are coarser and more plebeian.
Yet mark my words, for I read the stars,
 And trace the future in yonder sky;
To the right are wars and rumours of wars,
 To the left are peace and prosperity.
Fear naught. The world shall never detect
 The cloven hoof, so carefully hid
By the scholar so staid and circumspect,
 So wise for once to do as he's bid.
Remember what pangs come year by year
 For opportunity that has fled;
And Thora in ignorance.

Hugo: Name not her!
I am sorely tempted to strike thee dead!

Orion:
Nay, I hardly think you will take my life,
 The angel Michael was once my foe;
He had a little the best of our strife,
 Yet he never could deal so stark a blow.

SCENE — A Chamber in the Nuns' Apartments of the Convent.

AGATHA and URSULA.

Agatha:
My sire in my childhood pledged my hand
 To Hugo — I know not why —
They were comrades then, 'neath the Duke's command,
 In the wars of Lombardy.
I thought, ere my summers had turned sixteen,
 That mine was a grievous case;
Save once, for an hour, I had never seen
 My intended bridegroom's face;
And maidens vows of their own will plight.
 Unknown to my kinsfolk all
My love was vowed to a Danish knight,

A guest in my father's hall.
His foot fell lightest in merry dance,
　His shaft never missed the deer;
He could fly a hawk, he could wield a lance,
　Our wildest colt he could steer.
His deep voice ringing through hall or glen
　Had never its match in song;
And little was known of his past life then,
　Or of Dorothea's wrong.
I loved him — Lady Abbess, I know
　That my love was foolish now;
I was but a child five years ago,
　And thoughtless as bird on bough.
One evening Hugo the Norman came,
　And, to shorten a weary tale,
I fled that night (let me bear the blame)
　With Harold by down and dale.
He had mounted me on a dappled steed,
　And another of coal-black hue
He rode himself; and away at speed
　We fled through mist and dew.

Of miles we had ridden some half a score,
　We had halted beside a spring,
When the breeze to our ears through the still night bore
　A distant trample and ring;
We listen'd one breathing space, and caught
　The clatter of mounted men,
With vigour renewed by their respite short
　Our horses dash'd through the glen.
Another league, and we listen'd in vain;
　The breeze to our ears came mute;
But we heard them again on the spacious plain,
　Faint tidings of hot pursuit.
In the misty light of a moon half hid
　By the dark or fleecy rack,
Our shadows over the moorland slid,
　Still listening and looking back.
So we fled (with a cheering word to say
　At times as we hurried on),
From sounds that at intervals died away,
　And at intervals came anon.
Another league, and my lips grew dumb,

And I felt my spirit quailing,
For closer those sounds began to come,
And the speed of my horse was failing.
"The grey is weary and lame to boot,"
 Quoth Harold; "the black is strong,
And their steeds are blown with their fierce pursuit,
 What wonder! our start was long.
Now, lady, behind me mount the black,
 The double load he can bear;
We are safe when we reach the forest track,
 Fresh horses and friends wait there."
Then I sat behind him and held his waist,
 And faster we seemed to go
By moss and moor; but for all our haste
 Came the tramp of the nearing foe.
A dyke through the mist before us hover'd,
 And, quicken'd by voice and heel,
The black overleap'd it, stagger'd, recover'd;
 Still nearer that muffled peal.
And louder on sward the hoof-strokes grew,
 And duller, though not less nigh,
On deader sand; and a dark speck drew
 On my vision suddenly,
And a single horseman in fleet career,
 Like a shadow appear'd to glide
To within six lances' lengths of our rear,
 And there for a space to bide.
Quoth Harold, "Speak, has the moon reveal'd
His face?" I replied, "Not so!
Yet 'tis none of my kinsfolk." Then he wheel'd
 In the saddle and scanned the foe,
And mutter'd, still gazing in our wake,
 "'Tis he; now I will not fight
The brother again, for the sister's sake,
 While I can escape by flight."
"Who, Harold?" I asked; but he never spoke.
 By the cry of the bittern harsh,
And the bull-frog's dull, discordant croak,
 I guess'd that we near'd the marsh;
And the moonbeam flash'd on watery sedge
 As it broke from a strip of cloud,
Ragged and jagged about the edge,
 And shaped like a dead man's shroud.

And flagg'd and falter'd our gallant steed,
 'Neath the weight of his double burden,
As we splash'd through water and crash'd through reed;
 Then the soil began to harden,
And again we gain'd, or we seem'd to gain,
 With our foe in the deep morass;
But those fleet hoofs thunder'd, and gain'd again,
 When they trampled the firmer grass,
And I cried, and Harold again look'd back,
 And bade me fasten mine eyes on
The forest, that loom'd like a patch of black
 Standing out from the faint horizon.
"Courage, sweetheart! we are saved," he said;
 "With the moorland our danger ends,
And close to the borders of yonder glade
 They tarry, our trusty friends."
Where the mossy uplands rise and dip
 On the edge of the leafy dell,
With a lurch, like the lurch of a sinking ship,
 The black horse toppled and fell.
Unharm'd we lit on the velvet sward,
 And even as I lit I lay,
But Harold uprose, unsheath'd his sword,
 And toss'd the scabbard away.
And spake through his teeth, "Good brother-in-law,
 Forbearance, at last, is spent;
The strife that thy soul hath lusted for
 Thou shalt have to thy soul's content!"
While he spoke, our pursuer past us swept,
 Ere he rein'd his war-horse proud,
To his haunches flung, then to the earth he leapt,
 And my lover's voice rang loud:
"Thrice welcome! Hugo of Normandy,
 Thou hast come at our time of need,
This lady will thank thee, and so will I,
 For the loan of thy sorrel steed!"

And never a word Lord Hugo said,
 They clos'd 'twixt the wood and the wold,
And the white steel flickered over my head
 In the moonlight calm and cold;
'Mid the feathery grasses crouching low,
 With face bow'd down to the dust,

I heard the clash of each warded blow,
  The click of each parried thrust,
And the shuffling feet that bruis'd the lawn,
  As they traversed here and there,
And the breath through the clench'd teeth heavily drawn
  When breath there was none to spare;
Sharp ringing sword play, dull, trampling heel,
  Short pause, spent force to regain,
Quick muffled footfall, harsh grating steel,
  Sharp ringing rally again;
They seem'd long hours, those moments fleet,
  As I counted them one by one,
Till a dead weight toppled across my feet,
  And I knew that the strife was done.

When I looked up, after a little space,
  As though from a fearful dream,
The moon was flinging on Harold's face
  A white and a weird-like gleam;
And I felt mine ankles moist and warm
  With the blood that trickled slow
From a spot on the doublet beneath his arm,
  From a ghastly gash on his brow;
I heard the tread of the sorrel's hoof
  As he bore his lord away;
They passed me slowly, keeping aloof,
  Like spectres, misty and grey.
I thought Lord Hugo had left me there
  To die, but it was not so;
Yet then for death I had little care,
  My soul seem'd numb'd by the blow;
A faintness follow'd, a sickly swoon,
  A long and a dreamless sleep,
And I woke to the light of a sultry noon
  In my father's castled keep.

And thus, Lady Abbess, it came to pass
  That my father vow'd his vow;
Must his daughter espouse the Church? Alas!
  Is she better or wiser now?
For some are feeble and others strong,
  And feeble am I and frail.
Mother! 'tis not that I love the wrong,

'Tis not that I loathe the veil,
But with heart still ready to go astray,
 If assail'd by a fresh temptation,
I could sin again as I sinned that day,
 For a girl's infatuation.
See! Harold, the Dane, thou say'st is dead,
 Yet I weep NOT BITTERLY;
As I fled with the Dane, so I might have fled
 With Hugo of Normandy.

Ursula:
My child, I advise no hasty vows,
 Yet I pray that in life's brief span
Thou may'st learn that our Church is a fairer spouse
 Than fickle and erring man;
Though fenced for a time by the Church's pale,
 When that time expires thou'rt free;
And we cannot force thee to take the veil,
 Nay, we scarce can counsel thee.

   Enter the ABBOT hastily.

Basil (the Abbot):
I am sorely stricken with shame and grief,
 It has come by the self-same sign,
A summons brief from the outlaw'd chief,
 Count Rudolph of Rothenstein.
Lady Abbess, ere worse things come to pass,
 I would speak with thee alone;
Alack and alas! for by the rood and mass
 I fear we are all undone.

SCENE — A Farm-house Near the Convent.

A Chamber furnished with writing materials. HUGO, ERIC, and THURSTON on one side; on the other OSRIC, RUDOLPH, and DAGOBERT.

Osric:
We have granted too much, ye ask for more;
I am not skill'd in your clerkly lore,

I scorn your logic; I had rather die
Than live like Hugo of Normandy:
I am a Norseman, frank and plain;
Ye must read the parchment over again.

Eric:
Jarl Osric, twice we have read this scroll.

Osric:
Thou hast read a part.

Eric: I have read the whole.

Osric:
Aye, since I attached my signature!

Eric:
Before and since!

Rudolph: Nay, of this be sure,
Thou hast signed; in fairness now let it rest.

Osric:
I had rather have sign'd upon Hugo's crest;
He has argued the question mouth to mouth
With the wordy lore of the subtle south;
Let him or any one of his band
Come and argue the question hand to hand.
With the aid of my battle-axe I will show
That a score of words are not worth one blow.

Thurston:
To the devil with thee and thy battle-axe;
I would send the pair of ye back in your tracks,
With an answer that even to thy boorish brain
Would scarce need repetition again.

Osric:
Thou Saxon slave to a milksop knight,
I will give thy body to raven and kite.

Thurston:
Thou liest; I am a freeborn man,

And thy huge carcase — in cubit and span
Like the giant's of Gath — 'neath Saxon steel,
Shall furnish the kites with a fatter meal.

Osric:
Now, by Odin!

Rudolph: Jarl Osric, curb thy wrath;
Our names are sign'd, our words have gone forth.

Hugo:
I blame thee, Thurston.

Thurston: And I, too, blame
Myself, since I follow a knight so tame!
          [Thurston goes out.]

Osric:
The Saxon hound, he said I lied!

Rudolph:
I pray thee, good Viking, be pacified.

Osric:
Why do we grant the terms they ask?
To crush them all were an easy task.

Dagobert:
That know'st thou not; if it come to war,
They are stronger, perhaps, than we bargain for.

Eric:
Jarl Osric, thou may'st recall thy words —
Should we meet again.

Osric: Should we meet with swords,
Thou, too, may'st recall them to thy sorrow.

Hugo:
Eric! we dally. Sir Count, good-morrow.

SCENE — The Guest Chamber of the Convent.

HUGO, ERIC, and ORION.

Eric:
Hugo, their siege we might have tried;
This place would be easier fortified
Than I thought at first; it is now too late,
They have cut off our access to the gate.

Hugo:
I have weigh'd the chances and counted the cost,
And I know by the stars that all is lost
If we take up this quarrel.

Eric: So let it be!
I yield to one who is wiser than me. (Aside.)
Nevertheless, I have seen the day
When the stars would scarcely have bade us stay.

   Enter the ABBOT, CYRIL, and other Monks.

Hugo:
Lord Abbot, we greet thee. Good fathers all,
We bring you greeting.

Orion (aside):   And comfort small.

Abbot:
God's benediction on you, my sons.

Hugo:
May He save you, too, from Norsemen and Huns!
Since the gates are beleaguer'd and walls begirt
By the forces of Osric and Dagobert;
'Tis a heavy price that the knaves demand.

Abbot:
Were we to mortgage the Church's land
We never could raise what they would extort.

Orion (aside):
The price is too long and the notice too short.

Eric:
And you know the stern alternative.

Abbot:
If we die we die, if we live we live;
God's will be done; and our trust is sure
In Him, though His chast'nings we endure.
Two messengers rode from here last night,
To Otto they carry news of our plight;
On my swiftest horses I saw them go.

Orion (aside):
Then his swiftest horses are wondrous slow.

Eric:
One of these is captive and badly hurt;
By the reckless riders of Dagobert
He was overtaken and well-nigh slain,
Not a league from here on the open plain.

Abbot:
But the other escap'd.

Eric: It may be so;
We had no word of him, but we know
That unless you can keep these walls for a day
At least, the Prince is too far away
To afford relief.

Abbot: Then a hopeless case
Is ours, and with death we are face to face.

Eric:
You have arm'd retainers.

Cyril (a Monk):   Aye, some half score;
And some few of the brethren, less or more,
Have in youth the brunt of the battle bided,
Yet our armoury is but ill provided.

Hugo:
We have terms of truce from the robbers in chief,
Though the terms are partial, the truce but brief;

To Abbess, to nuns, and novices all,
And to every woman within your wall,
We can offer escort, and they shall ride
From hence in safety whate'er betide.

Abbot:
What escort, Hugo, canst thou afford?

Hugo:
Some score of riders who call me lord
Bide at the farm not a mile from here,
Till we rejoin them they will not stir;
My page and armourer wait below,
And all our movements are watch'd by the foe.
Strict stipulation was made, of course,
That, except ourselves, neither man nor horse
Should enter your gates — they were keen to shun
The chance of increasing your garrison.

Eric:
I hold safe conduct here in my hand,
Signed by the chiefs of that lawless band;
See Rudolph's name, no disgrace to a clerk,
And Dagobert's scrawl, and Osric's mark;
Jarl signed sorely against his will,
With a scratch like the print of a raven's bill;
But the foe have muster'd in sight of the gate.
For another hour they will scarcely wait;
Bid Abbess and dame prepare with haste.

Hugo:
Lord Abbot, I tell thee candidly
There is no great love between thou and I,
As well thou know'st; but, nevertheless,
I would we were more, or thy foes were less.

Abbot:
I will summon the Lady Abbess straight.
          [The Abbot and Monks go out.]

Eric:
'Tis hard to leave these men to their fate,
Norsemen and Hun will never relent;

Their day of grace upon earth is spent.
> [Hugo goes out, followed by Orion.]

SCENE — The Corridor Outside the Guest Chamber.

HUGO pacing up and down. ORION leaning against the wall.

Hugo:
My day of grace with theirs is past.
I might have saved them; 'tis too late —
Too late for both. The die is cast,
  And I resign me to my fate.
    God's vengeance I await.

Orion:
The boundary 'twixt right and wrong
Is not so easy to discern;
And man is weak, and fate is strong,
  And destiny man's hopes will spurn,
    Man's schemes will overturn.

Hugo:
Thou liest, thou fiend! Not unawares
 The sinner swallows Satan's bait,
Nor pits conceal'd nor hidden snares
 Seeks blindly; wherefore dost thou prate
    Of destiny and fate?

Orion:
Who first named fate? But never mind,
 Let that pass by — to Adam's fall
And Adam's curse look back, and find
 Iniquity the lot of all,
    And sin original.

Hugo:
But I have sinn'd, repented, sinn'd,
 Till seven times that sin may be
By seventy multiplied; the wind
 Is constant when compared with me,
    And stable is the sea!

My hopes are sacrificed, for what?
 For days of folly, less or more,
For years to see those dead hopes rot,
 Like dead weeds scatter'd on the shore,
  Beyond the surfs that roar!

Orion:
The wiles of Eve are swift to smite;
 Aye, swift to smite and not to spare —
Red lips and round limbs sweet and white,
 Dark eyes and sunny, silken hair,
  Thy betters may ensnare.

Hugo:
Not so; the strife 'twixt hell and heaven
 I felt last night, and well I knew
The crisis; but my aid was given
 To hell. Thou'st known the crisis too,
  For once thou'st spoken true.

Having foretold it, there remains
 For grace no time, for hope no room;
Even now I seem to feel the pains
 Of hell, that wait beyond the gloom
  Of my dishonour'd tomb.

Thou who hast lived and died to save,
 Us sinners, Christ of Galilee!
Thy great love pardon'd and forgave
 The dying thief upon the tree,
  Thou canst not pardon me!

Dear Lord! hear Thou my latest prayer,
 For prayer must die since hope is dead;
Thy Father's vengeance let me bear,
 Nor let my guilt be visited
  Upon a guiltless head!

Ah! God is just! Full sure I am
He never did predestinate
Our souls to hell. Ourselves we damn —
        [To Orion, with sudden passion]
Serpent! I know thee now, too late;

Curse thee! Work out thy hate!

Orion:
I hate thee not; thy grievous plight
 Would move my pity, but I bear
A curse to which thy curse seems light!
Thy wrong is better than my right,
My day is darker than thy night;
 Beside the whitest hope I share
   How white is thy despair!

SCENE — The Chapel of the Convent.

URSULA, AGATHA, Nuns and Novices.

(Hymn of the Nuns):

Jehovah! we bless Thee,
   All works of Thine hand
Extol Thee, confess Thee;
   By sea and by land,
By mountain and river,
   By forest and glen,
They praise Thee for ever!
   And ever! Amen!

The heathen are raging
   Against Thee, O Lord!
The ungodly are waging
   Rash war against God!
Arise, and deliver
   Us, sheep of Thy pen,
Who praise Thee for ever!
   And ever! Amen!

Thou Shepherd of Zion!
   Thy firstlings didst tear
From jaws of the lion,
   From teeth of the bear;
Thy strength to deliver
   Is strong now as then.

We praise Thee for ever!
   And ever! Amen!

Thine arm hath delivered
   Thy servants of old,
Hath scatter'd and shiver'd
   The spears of the bold,
Hath emptied the quiver
   Of bloodthirsty men.
We praise Thee for ever!
   And ever! Amen!

Nathless shall Thy right hand
   Those counsels fulfil
Most wise in Thy sight, and
   We bow to Thy will;
Thy children quail never
   For dungeon or den,
They praise Thee for ever!
   And ever! Amen!

Though fierce tribulation
   Endure for a space,
Yet God! our salvation!
   We gain by Thy grace,
At end of life's fever,
   Bliss passing man's ken;
There to praise Thee for ever!
   And ever! Amen!

SCENE — The Guest Room of the Convent.

HUGO, ERIC, and ORION. Enter URSULA, AGATHA, and Nuns.

Ursula:
Hugo, we reject thine offers,
   Not that we can buy
Safety from the Church's coffers,
   Neither can we fly.
Far too great the price they seek is,
   Let their lawless throng

Come, we wait their coming; weak is
Man, but God is strong.

Eric:
Think again on our proposals:
 It will be too late
When the robbers hold carousals
 On this side the gate.

Ursula:
For myself I speak and others
 Weak and frail as I;
We will not desert our brothers
 In adversity.

Hugo (to the Nuns):
Does the Abbess thus advance her
Will before ye all?

A Nun:
We will stay.

Hugo: Is this thine answer,
 Agatha? The wall
Is a poor protection truly,
 And the gates are weak,
And the Norsemen most unruly.
 Come, then.

A Nun (to Agatha):   Sister, speak!

Orion (aside to Hugo):
Press her! She her fears dissembling,
 Stands irresolute;
She will yield — her limbs are trembling,
 Though her lips are mute.
      [A trumpet is heard without.]

Eric:
Hark! their savage war-horn blowing
 Chafes at our delay.

Hugo:
Agatha, we must be going.
 Come, girl!

Agatha (clinging to Ursula):   Must I stay?

Ursula:
Nay, my child, thou shalt not make me
 Judge; I cannot give
Orders to a novice.

Agatha: Take me,
 Hugo! Let me live!

Eric (to Nuns):
Foolish women! will ye tarry,
 Spite of all we say?

Hugo:
Must we use our strength and carry
 You by force away?

Ursula:
Bad enough thou art, Sir Norman,
 Yet thou wilt not do
This thing. Shame! — on men make war, man,
 Not on women few.

Eric:
Heed her not — her life she barters,
 Of her free accord,
For her faith; and, doubtless, martyrs
 Have their own reward.

Ursula:
In the Church's cause thy father
 Never grudged his blade —
Hugo, did he rue it?

Orion: Rather!
 He was poorly paid.

Hugo:
Abbess, this is not my doing;
 I have said my say;
How can I avert the ruin,
 Even for a day,
Since they count two hundred fairly,
 While we count a score;
And thine own retainers barely
 Count a dozen more?

Agatha (kneeling to Ursula):
Ah! forgive me, Lady Abbess,
 Bless me ere I go;
She who under sod and slab is
 Lying, cold and low,
Scarce would turn away in anger
 From a child so frail;
Not dear life, but deadly danger,
 Makes her daughter quail.

Hugo:
Eric, will those faces tearful
 To God's judgment seat
Haunt us?

Eric: Death is not so fearful.

Hugo: No, but life is sweet —
Sweet for once, to me, though sinful.

Orion (to Hugo):   Earth is scant of bliss;
Wisest he who takes his skinful
 When the chance is his.

(To Ursula):
Lady Abbess! stay and welcome
 Osric's savage crew;
Yet when pains of death and hell come,
 Thou thy choice may'st rue.

Ursula (to Orion):
What dost thou 'neath roof-trees sacred?
 Man or fiend, depart!

Orion:
Dame, thy tongue is sharp and acrid,
  Yet I bear the smart.

Ursula (advancing and raising up a crucifix):
I conjure thee by this symbol
  Leave us!
        [Orion goes out hastily.]

Hugo: Ha! the knave,
He has made an exit nimble;
  Abbess! thou art brave.
Yet once gone, we're past recalling,
  Let no blame be mine.
See, thy sisters' tears are falling
  Fast, and so are thine.

Ursula:
Fare you well! The teardrop splashes
  Vainly on the ice.
Ye will sorrow o'er our ashes
  And your cowardice.

Eric:
Sorry am I, yet my sorrow
  Cannot alter fate;
Should Prince Otto come to-morrow,
  He will come too late.

Hugo:
Nay, old comrade, she hath spoken
  Words we must not hear;
Shall we pause for sign or token —
  Taunted twice with fear?
Yonder, hilt to hilt adjusted,
Stand the swords in which we trusted
Years ago. Their blades have rusted,
  So, perchance, have we.
Ursula! thy words may shame us,
Yet we once were counted famous,
Morituri, salutamus,
  Aut victuri, te!   [They go out.]

SCENE — The Outskirts of Rudolph's Camp.

RUDOLPH, OSRIC, and DAGOBERT. HUGO.
Rudolph:
Lord Hugo! thy speech is madness;
 Thou hast tax'd our patience too far;
We offer'd thee peace — with gladness,
 We gladly accept thy war.

Dagobert:
And the clemency we extended
 To thee and thine we recall;
And the treaty 'twixt us is ended —
 We are ready to storm the wall.

Osric:
Now tear yon parchment to tatters;
 Thou shalt make no further use
Of our safeguard; the wind that scatters
 The scroll shall scatter the truce.

Hugo:
Jarl Osric, to save the spilling
 Of blood, and the waste of life,
I am willing, if thou art willing,
 With thee to decide this strife;
Let thy comrades draw their force back;
 I defy thee to single fight,
I will meet thee on foot or horseback,
 And God shall defend the right.

Rudolph:
No single combat shall settle
 This strife; thou art overbold —
Thou hast put us all on our mettle,
 Now the game in our hands we hold.

Dagobert:
Our lances round thee have hover'd,
 Have seen where thy fellows bide;
Thy weakness we have discover'd,
 Thy nakedness we have spied.

Osric:
And hearken, knight, to my story —
 When sack'd are the convent shrines,
When the convent thresholds are gory,
 And quaff'd are the convent wines:
When our beasts with pillage are laden,
 And the clouds of our black smoke rise
From yon tower, one fair-haired maiden
 Is singled as Osric's prize.
I will fit her with chain and collar
 Of red gold, studded with pearls;
With bracelet of gold, Sir Scholar,
 The queen of my captive girls.

Hugo (savagely):
May the Most High God of battles
 The Lord and Ruler of fights,
Who breaketh the shield that rattles,
 Who snappeth the sword that smites,
In whose hands are footmen and horsemen,
 At whose breath they conquer or flee,
Never show me His mercy, Norseman!
 If I show mercy to thee.

Osric:
What, ho! art thou drunk, Sir Norman?
 Has the wine made thy pale cheek red?
Now, I swear by Odin and Thor, man,
 Already I count thee dead.

Rudolph:
I crave thy pardon for baulking
 The flood of thine eloquence,
But thou canst not scare us with talking,
 I therefore pray thee go hence.

Osric:
Though I may not take up thy gauntlet,
 Should we meet where the steel strikes fire,
'Twixt thy casque and thy charger's frontlet
 The choice will perplex thy squire.

Hugo:
When the Norman rowels are goading,
 When glitters the Norman glaive,
Thou shalt call upon Thor and Odin:
 They shall not hear thee nor save.
"Should we meet!" Aye, the chance may fall so,
 In the furious battle drive,
So may God deal with me — more, also!
 If we separate, both alive!

SCENE — The Court-yard of the Old Farm.

EUSTACE and other followers of HUGO and ERIC lounging about.
Enter THURSTON hastily, with swords under his arm.

Thurston:
Now saddle your horses and girth them tight,
And see that your weapons are sharp and bright.
Come, lads, get ready as fast as you can.

Eustace:
Why, what's this bustle about, old man?

Thurston:
Well, it seems Lord Hugo has changed his mind,
As the weathercock veers with the shifting wind;
He has gone in person to Osric's camp,
To tell him to pack up his tents and tramp!
But I guess he won't.

Eustace: Then I hope he will,
They are plenty to eat us, as well as to kill.

Ralph:
And I hope he won't — I begin to feel
A longing to moisten my thirsty steel.
        [They begin to saddle and make preparations
        for a skirmish.]

Thurston:
I've a couple of blades to look to here.

In their scabbards I scarcely could make them stir
At first, but I'll sharpen them both ere long.

A Man-at-arms:
Hurrah for a skirmish! Who'll give us a song?

Thurston (sings, cleaning and sharpening):
Hurrah! for the sword! I hold one here,
 And I scour at the rust and say,
'Tis the umpire this, and the arbiter,
 That settles in the fairest way;
For it stays false tongues and it cools hot blood,
 And it lowers the proud one's crest;
And the law of the land is sometimes good,
 But the law of the sword is best.
In all disputes 'tis the shortest plan,
 The surest and best appeal; —
What else can decide between man and man?

(Chorus of all):
 Hurrah! for the bright blue steel!

Thurston (sings):
Hurrah! for the sword of Hugo, our lord!
 'Tis a trusty friend and a true;
It has held its own on a grassy sward,
 When its blade shone bright and blue,
Though it never has stricken in anger hard,
 And has scarcely been cleansed from rust,
Since the day when it broke through Harold's guard
 With our favourite cut and thrust;
Yet Osric's crown will look somewhat red,
 And his brain will be apt to reel,
Should the trenchant blade come down on his head —

(Chorus of all):
 Hurrah! for the bright blue steel!

Thurston (sings):
Hurrah! for the sword of our ally bold,
 It has done good service to him;
It has held its own on an open wold,
 When its edge was in keener trim.

It may baffle the plots of the wisest skull,
  It may slacken the strongest limb,
Make the brains full of forethought void and null,
  And the eyes full of far-sight dim;
And the hasty hands are content to wait,
  And the knees are compelled to kneel,
Where it falls with the weight of a downstroke straight —

(Chorus of all):
  Hurrah! for the bright blue steel!

Thurston (sings):
Hurrah! for the sword — I've one of my own;
  And I think I may safely say,
Give my enemy his, let us stand alone,
  And our quarrel shall end one way;
One way or the other — it matters not much,
  So the question be fairly tried.
Oh! peacemaker good, bringing peace with a touch,
  Thy clients will be satisfied.
As a judge, thou dost judge — as a witness, attest,
  And thou settest thy hand and seal,
And the winner is blest, and the loser at rest —

(Chorus of all):
  Hurrah! for the bright blue steel!
          [Hugo and Eric enter during the last verse
          of the song.]

Hugo:
Boot and saddle, old friend,
Their defiance they send;
Time is short — make an end
   Of thy song.
Let the sword in this fight
Strike as hard for the right
As it once struck for might
   Leagued with wrong.

Ha! Rollo, thou champest
Thy bridle and stampest,
For the rush of the tempest
   Dost long?

Ho! the kites will grow fatter
On the corpses we scatter,
In the paths where we shatter
   Their throng.
Where Osric, the craven,
Hath reared the black raven
'Gainst monks that are shaven
   And cowl'd:
Where the Teuton and Hun sit,
In the track of our onset,
Will the wolves, ere the sunset,
   Have howl'd.

Retribution is good,
They have revell'd in blood,
Like the wolves of the wood
   They have prowl'd.
Birds of prey they have been,
And of carrion unclean,
And their own nests (I ween)
   They have foul'd.

Eric:
Two messengers since
Yestermorn have gone hence,
And ere long will the Prince
   Bring relief.
Shall we pause? — they are ten
To our one, but their men
Are ill-arm'd, and scarce ken
   Their own chief;
And for this we give thanks:
Their disorderly ranks,
If assail'd in the flanks,
   Will as lief
Run as fight — loons and lords.

Hugo:
Mount your steeds! draw your swords!
Take your places! My words
   Shall be brief:
Ride round by the valley,
Through pass and gorge sally —

The linden trees rally
   Beneath.
Then, Eric and Thurston,
Their ranks while we burst on,
Try which will be first on
   The heath.

(Aside)
Look again, mother mine,
Through the happy starshine,
For my sins dost thou pine?
   With my breath,
See! thy pangs are all done,
For the life of thy son:
Thou shalt never feel one
   For his death.

        [They all go out but Hugo, who lingers to tighten
        his girths. Orion appears suddenly in the gateway.]

Orion:
Stay, friend! I keep guard on
Thy soul's gates; hold hard on
Thy horse. Hope of pardon
   Hath fled!
Bethink once, I crave thee,
Can recklessness save thee?
Hell sooner will have thee
   Instead.

Hugo:
Back! My soul, tempest-toss'd,
Hath her Rubicon cross'd,
She shall fly — saved or lost!
   Void of dread!
Sharper pang than the steel,
Thou, oh, serpent! shalt feel,
Should I set the bruised heel
   On thy head.
       [He rides out.]

SCENE — A Room in the Convent Tower Overlooking the Gate.

URSULA at the window.   AGATHA and Nuns crouching or kneeling in a corner.

Ursula:
See, Ellinor! Agatha! Anna!
 While yet for the ladders they wait,
Jarl Osric hath rear'd the black banner
 Within a few yards of the gate;
It faces our window, the raven,
 The badge of the cruel sea-kings,
That has carried to harbour and haven
 Destruction and death on its wings.
Beneath us they throng, the fierce Norsemen,
 The pikemen of Rudolph behind
Are mustered, and Dagobert's horsemen
 With faces to rearward inclined;
Come last, on their coursers broad-chested,
 Rough-coated, short-pastern'd and strong,
Their casques with white plumes thickly crested,
 Their lances barb-headed and long:
They come through the shades of the linden,
 Fleet riders and war-horses hot:
The Normans, our friends — we have sinn'd in
 Our selfishness, sisters, I wot —
They come to add slaughter to slaughter,
 Their handful can ne'er stem the tide
Of our foes, and our fate were but shorter
 Without them. How fiercely they ride!
And "Hugo of Normandy!" "Hugo!"
 "A rescue! a rescue!" rings loud,
And right on the many the few go!
 A sway and a swerve of the crowd!
A springing and sparkling of sword-blades!
 A crashing and 'countering of steeds!
And the white feathers fly 'neath their broad blades
 Like foam-flakes! the spear-shafts like reeds!

A Nun (to Agatha):
Pray, sister!

Agatha: Alas! I have striven
To pray, but the lips move in vain
When the heart with such terror is riven.
Look again, Lady Abbess! Look again!

Ursula:
As leaves fall by wintry gusts scatter'd,
  As fall by the sickle ripe ears,
As the pines by the whirlwind fall shatter'd,
  As shatter'd by bolt fall the firs —
To the right hand they fall, to the left hand
  They yield! They go down! they give back!
And their ranks are divided and cleft, and
  Dispers'd and destroy'd in the track!
Where, stirrup to stirrup, and bridle
  To bridle, down-trampling the slain!
Our friends, wielding swords never idle,
  Hew bloody and desperate lane
Through pikemen, so crowded together
  They scarce for their pikes can find room,
Led by Hugo's gilt crest, the tall feather
  Of Thurston, and Eric's black plume!

A Nun (to Agatha):
Pray, sister!

Agatha: First pray thou that heaven
Will lift this dull weight from my brain,
That crushes like crime unforgiven.
Look again, Lady Abbess! Look again!

Ursula:
Close under the gates men are fighting
  On foot where the raven is rear'd!
'Neath that sword-stroke, through helm and skull smiting,
  Jarl Osric falls, cloven to the beard!
And Hugo, the hilt firmly grasping,
  His heel on the throat of his foe,
Wrenches back. I can hear the dull rasping,
  The steel through the bone grating low!

And the raven rocks! Thurston has landed
 Two strokes, well directed and hard,
On the standard pole, wielding, two-handed,
 A blade crimson'd up to the guard.
Like the mast cut in two by the lightning,
 The black banner topples and falls!
Bewildering! back-scattering! affright'ning!
 It clears a wide space next the walls.

A Nun (to Agatha):
Pray, sister!

Agatha: Does the sinner unshriven,
 With naught beyond this life to gain,
Pray for mercy on earth or in heaven?
 Look again, Lady Abbess! Look again!

Ursula:
The gates are flung open, and straightway,
 By Ambrose and Cyril led on,
Our own men rush out through the gateway;
 One charge, and the entrance is won!
No! our foes block the gate and endeavour
 To force their way in! Oath and yell,
Shout and war-cry wax wilder than ever!
 Those children of Odin fight well;
And my ears are confused by the crashing,
 The jarring, the discord, the din;
And mine eyes are perplex'd by the flashing
 Of fierce lights that ceaselessly spin;
So when thunder to thunder is calling,
 Quick flash follows flash in the shade,
So leaping and flashing and falling,
 Blade flashes and follows on blade!
While the sward, newly plough'd, freshly painted,
 Grows purple with blood of the slain,
And slippery! Has Agatha fainted?

Agatha:
Not so, Lady Abbess! Look again!

Ursula:
No more from the window; in the old years

I have look'd upon strife. Now I go
To the court-yard to rally our soldiers
As I may — face to face with the foe.
   [She goes out.]

SCENE — A Room in the Convent.

THURSTON seated near a small fire.

  Enter EUSTACE.

Eustace:
We have come through this skirmish with hardly a scratch.

Thurston:
And without us, I fancy, they have a full batch
Of sick men to look to. Those robbers accurs'd
Will soon put our soundest on terms with our worst.
Nathless I'd have bartered, with never a frown,
Ten years for those seconds when Osric went down.
Where's Ethelwolf?

Eustace: Dying.

Thurston: And Reginald?

Eustace: Dead.
And Ralph is disabled, and Rudolph is sped.
He may last till midnight — not longer. Nor Tyrrel,
Nor Brian will ever see sunrise.

Thurston: That Cyril,
The monk, is a very respectable fighter.

Eustace:
Not bad for a monk. Yet our loss had been lighter
Had he and his fellows thrown open the gate
A little more quickly. And now, spite of fate,
With thirty picked soldiers their siege we might weather,
But the Abbess is worth all the rest put together.
   [Enter Ursula.]

Thurston:
Here she comes.

Ursula: Can I speak with your lord?

Eustace: 'Tis too late,
He was dead when we carried him in at the gate.

Thurston:
Nay, he spoke after that, for I heard him myself;
But he won't speak again, he must lie on his shelf.

Ursula:
Alas! is he dead, then?

Thurston: As dead as St. Paul.
And what then? to-morrow we, too, one and all,
Die, to fatten these ravenous carrion birds.
I knelt down by Hugo and heard his last words:
"How heavy the night hangs — how wild the waves dash;
Say a mass for my soul — and give Rollo a mash."

Ursula:
Nay, Thurston, thou jestest.

Thurston: Ask Eric. I swear
We listened and caught every syllable clear.

Eustace:
Why, his horse was slain, too.

Thurston: 'Neath the linden trees grey,
Ere the onset, young Henry rode Rollo away;
He will hasten the Prince, and they may reach your gate
To-morrow — though to-morrow for us is too late.
Hugo rode the boy's mare, and she's dead — if you like —
Disembowel'd by the thrust of a freebooter's pike.

Eustace:
Neither Henry nor Rollo we ever shall see.

Ursula:
But we may hold the walls till to-morrow.

Thurston: Not we.
In an hour or less, having rallied their force,
They'll storm your old building — and take it, of course,
Since of us, who alone in war's science are skill'd,
One-third are disabled, and two-thirds are kill'd.

Ursula:
Art thou hurt?

Thurston: At present I feel well enough,
But your water is brackish, unwholesome and rough;
Bring a flask of your wine, dame, for Eustace and I,
Let us gaily give battle and merrily die.
            [Enter Eric, with arm in sling.]

Eric:
Thou art safe, Lady Abbess! The convent is safe!
To be robbed of their prey how the ravens will chafe!
The vanguard of Otto is looming in sight!
At the sheen of their spears, see! thy foemen take flight,
Their foremost are scarce half a mile from the wall.

Thurston:
Bring the wine, lest those Germans should swallow it all.

SCENE — The Chapel of the Convent.

Dirge of the Monks:
Earth to earth, and dust to dust,
 Ashes unto ashes go.
Judge not. He who judgeth just,
 Judgeth merciful also.
Earthly penitence hath fled,
 Earthly sin hath ceased to be;
Pile the sods on heart and head,
 Miserere Domine!

        Hominum et angelorum,
         Domine! precamur te
         Ut immemor sis malorum —
          Miserere Domine!

(Miserere!)

Will the fruits of life brought forth,
 Pride and greed, and wrath and lust,
Profit in the day of wrath,
 When the dust returns to dust?
Evil flower and thorny fruit
 Load the wild and worthless tree.
Lo! the axe is at the root,
 Miserere Domine!

>   Spes, fidesque, caritasque,
>   Frustra fatigant per se,
>   Frustra virtus, forsque, fasque,
>   Miserere Domine!
>   (Miserere!)

Fair without and foul within,
 When the honey'd husks are reft
From the bitter sweets of sin,
 Bitterness alone is left;
Yet the wayward soul hath striven
 Mostly hell's ally to be,
In the strife 'twixt hell and heaven,
 Miserere Domine!

>   Heu! heu! herba latet anguis —
>   Caro herba — carni vae —
>   Solum purgat, Christi sanguis,
>   Miserere Domine!
>   (Miserere!)

Pray that in the doubtful fight
 Man may win through sore distress,
By His goodness infinite,
 And His mercy fathomless.
Pray for one more of the weary,
 Head bow'd down and bended knee,
Swell the requiem, Miserere!
 Miserere Domine!

>   Bonum, malum, qui fecisti
>   Mali imploramus te,

Salve fratrem, causa Christi,
Miserere Domine!
    (Miserere!)

[End of Ashtaroth.]

CPSIA information can be obtained
at www.ICGtesting.com
Printed in the USA
LVHW090319280120
645023LV00003B/295

9 781714 246182